JOSHUA

School of Divinity

Gardner-Webb University

School

D1502500

—————————General Editor—————————
David A. Hubbard

—————————Old Testament Editor—————————
John D. W. Watts

—————————New Testament Editor—————————
Ralph P. Martin

UNDERSTANDING THE BASIC THEMES OF

JOSHUA

....

TRENT C. BUTLER

WORD PUBLISHING
Dallas · London · Vancouver · Melbourne

JOSHUA
Quick-Reference Bible Topics

Library of Congress Cataloging-in-Publication Data

Butler, Trent C.
    Joshua / Trent C. Butler.
        p.   cm. — (Quick-reference Bible topics)
    Includes bibliographical references and index.
    ISBN 0-8499-3247-5
    1. Bible. O.T. Joshua—Criticism, interpretation, etc.
I. Title. II. Series.
BS1295.2.B87   1991
222'.206—dc20
                                                                90-28364
                                                                CIP

Printed in the United States of America

1 2 3 4 9 RRD 9 8 7 6 5 4 3 2 1

CONTENTS

v

CONTENTS

FOREWORD

Finding the great themes of the books of the Bible is essential to the study of God's Word, and to the preaching and teaching of its truths. But these themes or ideas are often like precious gems; they lie beneath the surface and can only be discovered with some difficulty. The large commentaries are most useful to this discovery process, but they are not usually designed to help the student trace the important subjects within a given book of Scripture.

The *Quick-Reference Bible Topics* meet this need by bringing together, within a few pages, all of what is contained in a biblical volume on the subjects that are thought to be most significant to that volume. A companion series to the *Word Biblical Commentary*, these books seek to distill the theological essence of the biblical books as interpreted in the more technical series and to serve it up in ways that will enrich the preaching, teaching, worship, and discipleship of God's people.

Joshua is an up-beat narrative about the fulfillment of God's promises to an obedient people. It is the natural sequel to Deuteronomy. Dr. Trent Butler builds on his intensive research for his *Word Biblical Commentary* on Joshua to sketch the dominate themes of this intensely theological book.

This volume is sent forth in the hope that it will contribute to the vitality of God's people as we, too, try to occupy the promised land which God has for us.

Southern Baptist Theological Seminary Louisville, Kentucky	John D.W. Watts Old Testament Editor *Word Biblical Commentary* *Quick-Reference Bible Topics*

PREFACE

Learning biblical languages, researching for articles in scholarly journals, writing commentaries, all of the work the biblical scholar does has one ultimate goal—understanding the major topics Scripture teaches and helping the church understand and bring to life those topics.

In that sense this small volume represents the completion of the work on Joshua begun so many years ago and brought to major expression in the Word Biblical Commentary, Volume 7. The present book seeks to summarize the lessons learned from Joshua in writing the commentary and make those lessons available to a wider audience. All translations of Joshua in this book come from the commentary.

This volume is released to its wider audience with the prayer that it will help the church better understand the church's nature as God's people and help it to know its Lord. The volume is also released in gratitude to the editors and to numerous colleagues who have encouraged and inspired me to continue working in the book of Joshua. This book is due in no small part to my son Kevin and his assistance on the computer, and to my wife and her patience in letting me retire to the study for one more book.

Certainly other topics could be dealt with from Joshua. Also, the themes chosen for exposition here could be dealt with more clearly and comprehensively. I hope the present work will inspire readers to search Joshua and all of God's Word to find the truths he has taught his people and to determine how those truths should impact a believer's life. In this work, I have quoted from my own translation of Joshua as found in the volume of the Word Biblical Commentary. When reference is made to that book, Volume 7, it is abbreviated WBC 7:—(page number).

It is appropriate that I release this volume to the publisher at the Christmas season when one greater than Joshua took up the same Hebrew name and came to deliver God's people, not alone from enemies occupying the Promised Land, but from the ultimate enemy Sin, thus giving us salvation that reaches into the promised world to come. I release this manuscript with the prayer that it may help its readers face anew the call to commitment to be loyal people of the Lord in, over, and above history, and that it may call forth faith to know and follow because "I will put my laws into their minds, and I will write them upon their hearts. And I will be their God, and they shall be my people" (Heb 8:10 NASB).

Trent C. Butler
Brentwood, Tennessee

INTRODUCTION

The assignment: write a brief study on the themes of the book
of Joshua. This raises a probing question: How does one discover themes that are both important within the narrative
structure of Joshua and are of interest to readers approaching
the twenty-first century? The task calls for research into the
nature of biblical narrative and sensitivity to the concerns of
the modern church and world.

Research into biblical narrative literature has only recently
begun to ask questions concerning how to determine and define
narrative themes. Final answers are not yet available. Individual
scholars have proposed numerous methods of approach to biblical themes. Thus we are compelled to describe our approach
to biblical narrative as we begin this volume. The following
lines will sketch one possible method for determining which
themes are important within the narrative structure of biblical
literature. We will then apply the method to the book of Joshua
to determine significant themes. The remaining chapters will
take up each theme and trace its meaning within the book with
occasional references to the modern situation.

Method of approach

The type of literature

To know the themes of a piece of literature, we must know the kind of literature with which we are dealing. We will expect different things from satire, comedy, biography, court records, personal letters, and historical research. Most often, the type of literature will reveal the major theme of a book. A salvation oracle from a prophet or priest requires us to deal with the topic of salvation. A hymn of praise points to the topics of praise and worship. A letter calls forth the theme of relationships between the writer and recipients. An apocalyptic work makes investigation of persecution and future hope paramount.

The list could be extended indefinitely. The point is clear. The major theme of a work is more than the sum of major vocabulary items the writer used. A salvation oracle may never use the word *salvation*. A hymn may not explicitly mention worship. No one vocabulary item will define the relationship between writer and recipient of a letter. Only knowledge of the type of literature can give the necessary information to lead to the literary work's major theme.

The literary structure

The type of literature represents a general category with many individual literary works within the category. Comparing the individual works and finding their common elements and intention lets us define the category. Part of the definition will include general structural elements which recur in most pieces of literature that belong to the literary type. Thus a lament may be described as having the following elements: address to God, statement of the complaint, expression of trust in God's help, plea for God's help in the specific situation, description of enemies, and a concluding vow to praise and honor God for deliverance.[1]

Such general structural elements of a literary type find specific form in the individual work of literature. The structure of the individual work gives clues as to the major themes. Where the work varies from the usual structural elements of the literary type, where it creates new elements, where it repeats or otherwise gives special emphasis to elements, what it places in the introduction and conclusion—all these elements of literary structure provide strong evidence of the major theme of the work.

In one way or another the specific structure will point to the major point of discussion between author and audience, will show how various sides respond to the point of discussion, and will describe the author's solution to the situation. The author's solution will either affirm and expand that of the audience, or it will modify or deny that of the audience. Important topics appear both at the point of affirmation and at the point(s) of denial. This means an author can have both negative and positive themes. Such topics come to light as we study the literary structure of the individual work.

Vocabulary and vocabulary fields

A topic can appear without ties to specific vocabulary as noted above, but a writer often highlights a theme by repeating certain key terms and phrases. The writer may use such terms because the audience uses them and finds strong emotional support in them. The writer may make very subtle or not so subtle shifts in meaning by placing these important terms in new contexts or by illustrating them in ways that give new definitions to old words. Vocabulary items, as such, do not constitute literary or theological themes. Rather, literary themes emerge from (1) the interaction among related vocabulary items and (2) the distinctions between the audience's understanding of these vocabulary items and the author's definition of those items. Themes emerge from vocabulary or word study not simply through classical dictionary definitions but through examination of their functions in the context of the literary work and in the social/theological context of the audience.

Characterization

Characterization creates literary themes. A writer, even of history, chooses heroes and villains carefully. Heroes become in some sense role models for the audience. The goals the hero seeks to attain, the hero's actions, the hero's speeches, and the hero's final fate combine to set forth an understanding of human purpose and destiny. Similar portrayal of the villain(s) provides the negative theme(s). Similarly, heroic goals unfulfilled and a villain's goals undefeated may represent literary themes specifically directed to the new generation represented by the audience.

Transition points

Delay in action and transition points often allow the author to interject important topical statements. These may appear in different forms: repeated ritual acts; long speeches; summary statements; character description; theological definitions. Such statements allow the author to address the contemporary audience as well as to make historical descriptions. Precisely at such transition points in the narrative, we expect to discover the points of tension which the author addresses and the options which the reading or listening audience faces.

Larger literary context

The larger literary context serves as a checkpoint by which to judge whether the criteria stated above have been used correctly to isolate the writer's themes. If the context under immediate consideration is part of a larger literary whole, then the topics emphasized will prove to be significant within the larger literary work. Topics from the smaller context not taken up in the larger context should not be emphasized as major themes by modern study. Thus, in the present study of the book of Joshua, we must concentrate on topics which stretch forward through the Former Prophets—Judges, Samuel, Kings. We may also want to see how Joshua carries forward themes from its immediate literary predecessor—the Pentateuch (Genesis through Deuteronomy). From the standpoint of evangelical Christianity, we will want to look at an even larger context, that of the New Testament. How does the New Testament expand the themes of Joshua in light of the supreme revelation in Jesus Christ?

Limits

Our own literary work cannot be infinite and endless. We must choose to examine only certain topics, not all those found in Joshua. We will want to examine those themes that (1) appear to have major significance in the book of Joshua, (2) either are unique to Joshua in the biblical literature, on the one hand, or appear to be significant in light of the New Testament, and (3) seem to have the potential to speak to significant needs of the contemporary church and world. Such a statement must be modified somewhat. We must not eliminate a statement simply because we see no potential meaning for the modern world, for a major theme in biblical literature stands there precisely through the working of the Holy Spirit and has strong potential for meaning as the Spirit continues to work in the life of the church and its individual members. Still, we seek to work with topics for which modern application is most apparent in hopes of being an instrument of the Spirit in speaking to the lives of his people.

Themes in Joshua

The method described could be extended, adding other literary techniques to refine the method and establish an even longer list of themes. We will use these six methodological criteria to determine themes in the book of Joshua.

Joshua as biography

Joshua represents a complex type of literature. It is closely associated with Judges, Samuel, and Kings—books whose subject matter is historical events and persons. Thus, our first impression is to classify the book as history writing and define history writing to determine the overarching themes of Joshua. This approach is only a first step, however. History writing is too large a category to deal with. Royal annals, chronicles, personal diaries, oral traditions, political propaganda . . . one can go on and on with various literary types that belong to the major category of history writing. We must ask what kind of history writing the book of Joshua represents. In so doing, we must consider the Jews' traditional classification of Joshua as part of the Former Prophets.

In a real sense, Joshua is history writing from a prophetic perspective. That is, the book of Joshua does not simply choose selected historical facts and line them up in chronological order. Joshua expects those historical facts to provide insight into the meaning of life in God's world under God's direction. It expects God's people to understand life in the present with him in light of life in the past with him. Similarly, it points to hope for life in the future because of the reality of a life of hope in the past. The facts of past history become a literary tool for the inspired writer to provide a spiritual message for the present. Only because the book of Joshua has this inspired prophetic element do we continue to seek out its themes and employ those themes to guide our life under God.

To say the book of Joshua has a prophetic element or is prophetic history writing still does not define its literary type. Prophecy can be presented in the familiar collections of oracles or prophetic speeches that we see in Isaiah or Micah. It can be presented in the question and answer mode of Habakkuk, the narrative style of Jonah, the woes of Amos or Nahum, the priestly style of Malachi, or the apocalyptic combination of narrative and vision of Daniel. Prophecy is more a personal function than a literary type. We still must ask the literary nature of the prophetic history in the book of Joshua.

To determine literary structure, we must look at the individual elements of structure in the book of Joshua. How can we in one sentence describe each of the sections of Joshua? The following picture develops.[2]

1:1–9	Joshua is inducted into Moses' office.
1:10–18	Joshua functions as commander of Israel and of East Jordan troops.
2:1–24	Joshua sends spies to see the land; they report back to him.
3:1–5:1	Joshua directs the crossing of the Jordan and receives the renown of Moses.
5:2–9	Joshua sanctifies the negligent people by circumcising them.
5:10–12	The sanctified people celebrate Passover.
5:13–15	Joshua passes the test administered by the Prince of the Host of Yahweh.
6:1–27	Jericho is given into Joshua's hands.
7:1–5	Joshua leads a futile attack against Ai after Achan's sin and the spies' foolish advice.
7:6–9	Joshua leads a public lamentation ceremony.
7:10–26	Joshua leads a public trial at Yahweh's command.
8:1–29	Joshua captures Ai.
8:30–35	Joshua builds an altar and leads a covenant ceremony according to the law of Moses.

20:1–9	Joshua obeys Yahweh as given in Moses' commands and sets up cities of refuge.
21:1–42	Eleazar and Joshua obey Yahweh's will as given in Moses' commands and provide cities for the landless Levites.
21:43–45	Yahweh fulfilled all His promises.
22:1–8	Joshua sends the obedient eastern tribes home across Jordan.
22:9–34	Phinehas, the priest, settles an altar dispute between eastern and western tribes.
23:1–16	Joshua delivers his farewell sermon, admonishing the tribes to obedience.
24:1–28	Joshua leads tribes in covenant commitment to Yahweh.
24:9–23	Joshua, Joseph, and Eleazar are buried.

Looking at the individual units reveals quite clearly that the narrative structure of the book of Joshua has one center. Joshua is the actor on stage at every important juncture. The book of Joshua tells the story of Joshua. The subject of the lead sentences of the book of Joshua is Joshua. The further the book continues, the greater the fame and glory of Joshua. The narrative structure of the book does not concentrate so much on conquest and land distribution as it does on the person and work of Joshua.

The concentration of the narrative structure is not total, however. At important points, Joshua disappears briefly. He does not explicitly lead the Passover celebration (5:10–12), but he had prepared Israel to celebrate Passover by circumcising the men. Joshua heard a word from Yahweh or initiated an action to begin each major section (1:1; 2:1; 3:1; 4:1; 5:2; 6:2) until chapter 7. There, the sons of Israel (7:1)—represented in the one man Achan—initiated the action. Only under this heading did Joshua undertake a futile action (7:2). Even then, Joshua's actions under God's leadership finally corrected the situation. Again, Joshua is the major actor (8:1, 30) or the one causing the enemies' actions (9:1–3) until a major wrong is committed. Then the men of Israel accept the Gibeonites' evidence, having failed to inquire of Yahweh (9:14). Joshua then made peace and signed an agreement to let the Gibeonites live (9:15). Finally, Joshua graciously rescued the Gibeonites from the sons of Israel (9:26).

Joshua again took first place in the allotment of the land (13:1), but Eleazar also shared the spotlight, even being mentioned before Joshua (14:1; 17:4; 19:51). Still, when an action occurred, the actor was Joshua (14:13; 15:13; 17:14–18). This continued in chapter 20, where Joshua set up the cities of refuge; but in chapter 21 Eleazar appeared again beside Joshua. In 22:2 Joshua acted alone, dismissing the eastern tribes and preaching to them to be faithful to the law of Moses.

Suddenly in 22:10–34, Joshua disappeared. Phinehas, the priest, occupied center stage to settle the altar dispute between east and west. Can we explain Joshua's lapses from the stage? Perhaps! In the early chapters Joshua disappeared in the time of blame. The narration shifts the center of attention away from Joshua only when Israel violates the law of Moses. In the second half of the book, Joshua is called to share the central actions with the priest when cultic actions take place at a worship center. When the problem becomes totally cultic, the priest alone is involved. Thus, context appears to dictate when Joshua must yield the central position to another character. Such brief exits do not change the central structure of the book. They only show Joshua's willingness to work with other officials and to acknowledge the limits of his role. The book remains a story about Joshua, the leader par excellence. In some sense the literary type of the book is biography, documenting the life of a leader in Israel after Moses. That biography is then structured in a particular way to make its unique points and present its unique themes.

Showing that Joshua is a biography of a leader leads us far down the path to the book's major themes. A biography sets up the central figure as a person of importance whose example becomes a role model to follow or to avoid. A biography forces us to look at personal themes rather than abstract themes. In this case the biography of a leader means we must look at personal leadership themes. We must determine what makes Joshua a leader, what tasks a leader faces, where a leader gets leadership in accomplishing those tasks, and how a leader faces failure as well as success. To know exactly how to do this, we must go still further. We must follow the outline of the method given above to better define the themes inherent in a biography of a leader.

Literary structure of the biography

Biography can be a complex genre using many literary techniques to give historical perspective and character development of the central character and several other major personalities. Flashbacks, monologs, personal descriptions, conversations, dreams, personal reflections, moving back and forth among several contemporaneous events, and other complex literary techniques allow biographers to delve deep into personality make-up and present psychological analysis of people in all their complexity. The book of Joshua is much simpler in its techniques and much more direct in its structure. It describes the character's actions and presents the character in dialog, particularly in dialog with God. As elsewhere in the Ancient Near East, biography had the office and function of the person as its theme, not the personal character traits and emotions. Biography featured the public life rather than the private, personal affairs of its subject. Life and office became practically identical. Biography was much more interested in the typical that later generations could emulate and repeat rather than in individual fate.

In dealing with the public rather than the private person, biography often began with the public birth—the installation into office—not with the private birth to a mother. The installation report opening the biography often introduced the major themes taken up in the biography proper. Such topics include securing peace from external and internal enemies, establishing social justice within the nation, and preserving the purity of the cult.

Thus in the book of Joshua, the center of attention is Joshua and his office. The book begins with a report of his installation in office as leader of the conquest and of the division of the land. These functions establish peace with enemies externally and internally, setting up a society at rest, thus a society with social justice and a pure cult. The book tells how Joshua carried out these public functions. All private details—even names of family members—are passed over without mention. We do not meet Joshua, the individual person; we meet Joshua, the national leader. In his official function Joshua secures peace for the people and peace among the people. He lays the demands of the Law of Moses before the people to secure social justice. He delivers a divine ultimatum as to their choice of God, seeking to ensure the purity of the cult.

Structural elements easily separate the book of Joshua into distinct units. Chapter 1 initiates Joshua into his office and sets out the task facing Israel, including the tribes east of the Jordan. Chapters 2 through 5 show Joshua's effective leadership and make him and the people cultically ready to fulfill the mission God has set before them.

Chapters 6 through 11 show Joshua obediently overcoming all opposition to conquer the land. Chapter 12 summarizes the conquest and closes the first half of the book. Chapter 13 shows the second stage of Joshua's mission—apportioning the land west of Jordan as Moses had apportioned that east of Jordan. Joshua had to do this even though much of the promised land remained to be conquered. Chapters 14 through 17 show how land was provided for Judah, Ephraim, and Manasseh. Chapters 18 and 19 show how Joshua motivated the remaining 7 tribes to determine and possess their allotment.

Chapters 20 and 21 set up a just social system for inadvertent murderers and for landless priests. The second half of the book then finds its conclusion in the summary statement of 21:43–45. Joshua had solved the problems with external foes. Chapter 22 establishes internal peace among feuding tribes and sets forth the basic rule of cultic purity agreed to by all the people.

Chapters 23 and 24 conclude the book with Joshua's sermon and his leading Israel to renew the covenant with God. The biographical epilog (24:29–33) then reports Joshua's death and burial, the fulfillment of the promise to Joseph to bury his remains in the promised land, and the death and burial of Eleazar the priest.

The structure of Joshua thus can be outlined as follows:

I. The Introduction: Joshua's initiation as leader after and under Moses (1:1–18)

II. The Body: Joshua establishes external and internal rest (2:1–21:45)

   A. Joshua leads in conquest of the land (2:1–12:24)

     1. Joshua helps the people prepare for conquest (2:1–5:15)

     2. Joshua leads the people to conquer the land (6:1–11:15)

     3. Joshua's conquest summarized (11:16–12:24)

   B. Joshua and Eleazar demonstrate social justice in action distributing the land (13:1–19:51)

   C. Joshua establishes justice and peace for underprivileged (20:1–21:42)

   D. Summary: God fulfilled all his promises (21:43–45)

III. Conclusion: Joshua and Eleazar establish cultic purity (22:1–24:28)

   A. Joshua commissions the eastern tribes (22:1–6)

   B. Phinehas leads to cultic agreement among the tribes (22:7–34)

C. Joshua leads people to covenant agreement (23:1–
   24:28)
IV. Epilog: Leaders buried and promises kept (24:29–33)

The structure of the book of Joshua thus leads us to look at
seven basic themes:
(1) Leadership after Moses
(2) Rest
(3) The land
(4) Justice
(5) Pure worship
(6) Divine promises
(7) Covenant religion
The methodological areas studied below may provide further
themes or new structure for these themes.

Vocabulary fields of the book of Joshua

Special words punctuate the inspired biography of Joshua.
With these words, the author underlined themes the readers
needed to ponder. Using the outline above, words can be selected which recur frequently and which carry thematic weight
for the author. Obviously, some words will occur many times
without carrying thematic weight—such as "to be," "and,"
"have," "say"—and other words necessary to carry normal narrative along.
A vocabulary review shows that some words recur in all
sections of the book: "Yahweh," "Joshua," "Moses," "land,"
"giving," "possession/inheritance," "rest," "servant of Yahweh,"
"Reuben," and "Gad." Other words such as "Torah," "obey,"
"ban," "covenant," and "altar" influence some sections but not
all. Still other words—such as "ark of the covenant," "rebel,"
"loyal," "dread by the inhabitants"—play significant roles in
individual sections or even in isolated narratives, but do appear
in other sections of the book. Further study of transition points

in the book may help explain the diffusion and concentration of vocabulary items. For the moment, let us note that the vocabulary items of significance can be organized under a few categories:

1. Leadership	2. Land	3. Law
Joshua	Giving	Torah
Moses	Possession	Word
Great	Inheritance	Obey
Until this day	Rest	Commandment
	Oath to fathers	
	Ban	
	Land	
	Lot	

4. Loyalty	5. Lord
Covenant	Yahweh
Servant	With you
Reuben	Ark
Loyal	Wonders
Rebel	Anger
Faithful	

Characterization in the book of Joshua

Strangely for our taste, characterization does not play a strong role for the author of the biography of Joshua. This apparently results from the nature of Near Eastern biography with its emphasis on office more than on office-holder. The individual character traits of Joshua disappear behind the official of Moses carrying out the commands of Torah and the spoken words of Yahweh and thus accomplishing his mission. The author never takes time to step back from the action to describe Joshua or to picture Joshua in repose or in reflection. Rather, Joshua remains in constant action throughout the book's twenty-four chapters.

The simple-minded devotion to action shows the inspired writer's understanding of leadership of Israel after Moses. Leadership consists in obedient action much more than in developing a public image dominated by certain popular personality traits.

Transition points in the book of Joshua

Certain key transition sections sparkle with diamonds of theological truth in somewhat irregular intervals through the book of Joshua. Each of the individual conquest narratives as well as the other individual narratives of the book have important themes which a total study of Joshua must investigate, but the transitions show us where the author chose to place the narrative weight. At least the following elements stand out as compositional markers leading us down the path to the key themes of Joshua.

1. *Theological prologue: leader and people defined (1:1–18).* Here we find divine marching orders for Israelite leadership after Moses, the chain of command in Israel illustrated, and the call for national unity. The Israelite leader has a clear task—take the land; a sure guidebook—the Torah of Moses; and a reassuring promise—I am with you. He has other leaders to help him accomplish the task, and he has assurance from the tribes most tempted not to participate—they will obey his leadership.

2. *Cultic interlude: worship as the center of identity (8:30–35).* This passage shocks modern readers by intruding on the continuity of the conquest narratives. The story turns from war to worship, from Gilgal to Shechem, and from conquest to covenant. The author used the transition shock to call attention to important themes—place of worship, allegiance to Torah, chain of command, universal instruction in Torah, and fulfillment of Torah. Joshua must not be read as a simple book of holy war, conquest, and selfish grabbing of land. It must be seen rather as pointing to leadership after Moses in the light of the

Torah of Moses. Only after we have taken a break in the action to learn this lesson should we return to the action of conquest and learn the rest of the story.

3. *Theological summary: promises fulfilled (11:23).* Ten chapters (2–11) lay out the conquest narratives. One transitional verse gives the meaning. The major goal of the conquest narrative deals not with human activity and human achievement. Conquest narrative does not become a manual for future battle; nor does it become a universally valid theology of warfare. Conquest narrative points to God's faithfulness, to Israel's possession by grace, and to God's goal for his people—rest from battle.

4. *Theological review: the task ahead (13:1–7).* Narrative breaks the bonds of past history, pointing beyond itself to future goals. No leader dies without new fields to conquer. New tasks and new challenges stare each new generation and its leaders in the face. Joshua faced old age (note the artistic inclusion joining 13:1 and 23:1) with a large conquest task remaining. As so often in biblical narrative, the author used divine monolog to make this important transition.

Incompleteness and a task remaining did not mean Joshua had failed as leader. Rather, it called for new trust in God to fulfill new promises and for new commitment to the parallel task of distributing the land. Fair distribution took priority over total destruction of enemies and total conquest of land. (The first chapters of Judges return to this theme.)

5. *Theological acclamation: God is faithful (21:43–45).* Repetition among transition statements underlines the importance of a theme. The conquest summary underlined God's faithfulness (11:23). The distribution summary does the same. A task remaining and land unconquered do not detract from God's faithfulness. They only reassure the new generation called to cooperate with God in bringing new promises to fulfillment. God's people have no basis for complaint. God is perfectly faithful. His Word proves true in human history. No enemy threatens God. He defeats every one he faces when and how he chooses.

6. *A theological program: life with God anywhere (22:1–6)*. The speech of a hero can mark transition as easily as divine speech. When such speech forms a literary inclusion with previous transition material, as 22:1–6 does with 1:12–18, then the reader seeking important themes must certainly pay close attention to the passage. The literary signals are especially important for the modern reader here, for we are tempted to see 22:1–6 as an interlude preparing for the interesting story to follow. Thus, at the first reading, we pass over it without marking its thematic importance. As the author turned to the task of the future in 13:1–7, so the future stands in perspective here. The unity of God's people must endure the strains of rest even more than the stress of war. The unity of God's people must endure even the absence of symbols and of the rites of unity. The unity of God's people comes from obedience to the Torah of Moses. Such unity can be preserved no matter where God's people live and no matter what worship conveniences they are missing.

7. *Theological justification: leave Torah, lose land (23:1–16)*. Most narrative books have important introductory and concluding transition statements, moving into and out of the major story line. Joshua doubles up on the exit transition, presenting first the hero's concluding speech and then the concluding ritual (ch 24). Both point to the future. Past promises are secure (11:23; 21:43–45). Future promises stand tied to human commitment. The message reaches the people through the chain of command. The message calls for awareness of the past, knowledge of the task remaining, confidence in God to accomplish the task, commitment to obey God's Torah and to love him, and trust in God strong enough to avoid the temptation of other gods. The message centers on warning. Fulfillment of promises can turn to fulfillment of threats. Life in the land without Torah will mean life without the land.

8. *Theological hope: covenant with God (24:1–28)*. A unique covenant ceremony pairs with Joshua's farewell address to conclude the book of Joshua. This models Israel's hope for identity in all

ages. The story has featured fighting and land distribution. The conclusion features Joshua's intense efforts to bond Israel to God through covenant ritual and personal commitment. Again, the place is Shechem, as in the transition ritual at 8:30–35. The mediators are the officials in Joshua's chain of command. The introduction is historical review. The featured performer is not Joshua nor his armies, but Yahweh, the God who fights and forms Israel's history.

The conclusion is a call for absolute commitment to this God, a commitment that excludes all other commitments and that admits the impossible nature of fulfilling the commitment. The result is the covenant between Yahweh and Israel based on Torah. That is the basis for life in the inherited land.

These eight transition sections guide us to themes in Joshua. Taken together, they represent a call to unity among God's people in following God's Torah to be faithful members of God's covenant, resisting all temptations to follow other gods, and depending on God to complete the unfinished task through new leaders like Joshua. Meanwhile, God's people rest from battle, enjoying life in the land God has faithfully given in fulfillment of all his promises. God's faithfulness stands proven in history. The future will render a verdict on Israel's faithfulness. Stern, concluding warnings in the book of Joshua caution the reader not to be too optimistic concerning Israel's faithfulness or concerning God's leniency with an unfaithful people.

Larger literary context

A few general and quite apparent observations would be appropriate. The book of Joshua builds strongly on the foundation of Deuteronomy, a foundation based on a covenant structure of faithfulness to Torah centered in the Decalog (Deut 5). Deuteronomy looks for one people to serve one God at one sanctuary or face the covenant curses. Such service is a service of love of God and devotion to his word.[3]

Judges follows Joshua and provides the reverse side of life. As Joshua is the biography of a faithful leader in the shadow of Moses, so Judges is the biography of a faithless nation in the shadow of their sin because they lack faithful leadership and need a king.[4] First Samuel then shows God providing a king for his people; but the very first king foreshadows the history of kingship, being more willing to meet immediate needs with human actions than to meditate on Torah, understand God, and wait for his actions. The failed leadership of Saul contrasts with the pious leadership examples of Samuel before God and David waiting to come after him.[5] Second Samuel features God's covenant king for His covenant people. Here is the beginning of what Joshua could not provide—permanent leadership for God's people. Second Samuel gives for David what the book of Joshua did not give for Joshua—characterization. Precisely, that characterization separates David from Joshua, for it shows the weakness and sin of David, something never seen in Joshua.[6]

Joshua thus stands as the model for leadership in Israel, while David stands as the human example of leadership—strongly committed to Yahweh, yet fully involved in the world and its strong temptations. Here another nuance of leadership theology appears. Leadership is not condemned to destruction for occasional unfaithfulness. Joshua 24 had already noted the impossibility of total faithfulness. Rather, the condemnation of leadership comes only in Kings.

First and Second Kings show the demise of united Israel and the destruction of the two separated kingdoms.[7] Such destruction is not explained in terms of warfare and political/military strength. Destruction is explained in terms of leadership unfaithful to God's Torah. The precedent set by Joshua and by David was not enough. The covenant warnings of Deuteronomy and of Joshua 23–24 faded into ancient tradition which modern kings refused to believe. Saul's course of reliance on human strategy and the obvious need for strong actions in the face of crisis became the model for kingship in Israel and in Judah.

The example of Canaan and Phoenicia depending on various gods for various actions replaced the demand for a unified people at a unified worship place worshiping and trusting one God.

This short rehearsal of themes from Deuteronomy, Judges, Samuel, and Kings shows the themes isolated in Joshua represent themes of the larger context. Deuteronomy through Kings centers on leadership of the one people of God seeking to provide rest in the land through covenant faithfulness to the one God, a faithfulness seen in obedience to Torah.

The slow train named Method has reached its destination. The type of literature has raised LEADERSHIP as the pervading theme of Joshua. Structure has revealed *leadership after Moses, rest from battle, life in the land, justice, pure worship, divine promise,* and *covenant* as central themes. Vocabulary has pointed out *leadership, land, law, loyalty,* and *Lord* as organizing themes around which major vocabulary items can be studied. The transition statements focus on *leadership, unity, covenant, life in the land,* and *the call for faithfulness* to match God's faithfulness.

We will use the organizing categories of the vocabulary section as the organizing principle for the work that follows and will seek to study the themes of Joshua under those categories. These will all point us to one final question, the question we consider key to Joshua and to Old Testament theology as a whole, namely: Who are the people of God? We will address that question in a concluding epilog.

1

LEADERSHIP OF THE PEOPLE OF GOD

The biography of Joshua answers the basic question: What is the leader of God's people like? The word *leader* does not occur. No one narrative or transition section explicitly describes leadership. The central leader, Joshua, occupies no office known by later Israel. Still, literary type and structure show that leadership is the overarching theme of the book of Joshua. Study of the larger literary context only fortifies this conclusion. To study leadership is to study the person of Joshua, the demands placed on him, his actions, and his titles.

Moses, the shadow behind Israel's leaders

Leadership in the book of Joshua begins with Moses, not Joshua. Joshua is only the official or minister of Moses (1:1). He is not a slave or servant. He is a youthful page freely serving his master.[8] As such, Joshua had made many youthful mistakes. He went up the holy mountain with Moses (Exod 24:13). Coming down, Joshua reported to Moses that he heard the sound of war in the Israelite camp below (Exod 32:17), but Moses corrects his impression, noting that it was the sound of singing (v 18).

Then in the wilderness God sent his Spirit upon the elders near the Tent of Meeting, even two who stayed in the camp rather than go to the tent received the Spirit. Joshua protested, asking Moses to make them quit prophesying (Num 11:28), apparently an attempt to protect Moses' exclusive position. Moses corrected him, expressing his desire that all God's people could be prophets. He may also have been protecting the Tent of meeting as the place of revelation, since he apparently had a permanent position there (Exod 32:11).

Joshua 1 marked the transition point in Joshua's life and ministry. He moved from minister of Moses to the installed leader of God's people. Youthful mistakes of the past did not matter. It was time to forsake such defensive behavior and assume responsibility. Assuming leadership did not mean moving out of the shadow of Moses, however. Rather, for Joshua, it meant moving further into that shadow. Death did not remove Moses from the Israelite scene. Death only moved Moses' mode of leadership from mortal human leader to eternal director through the Word, the inspired Torah he left behind.

Every leader who came after Joshua would face the same situation. Leadership in Israel meant followship of the Torah of Moses. Joshua's first instructions from God did not concern military strategy; they concerned the leader's guidebook (1:7–8). Leadership in Israel meant devoted study of God's Word (compare Deuteronomy 17:18–20.) Such study was not to be in crisis, or of an intermittent nature. It was to be daily study. Only a leader devoted to Torah study could demand such study from the people. Only such a devoted leader could meet the criteria of Torah God uses to judge leaders (compare 2 Kings 17:34–40). Torah sparked renewal and hope for God's leader (compare 2 Kings 22–23).

Leadership for God's people is thus tied tightly to Torah, the Law of Moses. To be a leader is to be a follower of Moses and his Torah. The call to leadership was not a call to rebellion, to military coup, to the establishment of one's personal style and image. The call to leadership was a call to more of the same, to following the tradition, to staying on Torah's path without any deviation. The result would be courage, conviction, prudence, prosperity, and success—for devotion of Torah guaranteed the presence of God.

Leadership in the shadow of Moses set the model for servant-leadership, for Moses was the "servant of Yahweh" (Josh 1:1). This title placed Moses in a different category than Joshua. Joshua's title related him to Moses. He was Moses' official or minister (Josh 1:1). Moses' title related him to Yahweh as his servant. The title is not unique to the book of Joshua. Moses humbly, reverently appropriated the title to himself in seeking to decline God's call to leadership (Exod 4:10). In so doing he identified himself with a slave bought with money (Exod 13:3, 14).

The Exodus event climaxed with Israel recognizing that Moses was Yahweh's servant so that the people put their trust in him and in Yahweh (Exod 14:31). In so doing they used "servant" in an entirely different sense. "Servant" in this context meant a high government official or advisor to the king. The Hebrew term could be applied to Pharaoh's officials (Exod 5:15–16; 7:20; 9:20 and others). In his own eyes the meek Moses kneeled as God's slave. In the eyes of Israel he stood tall, earning their complete trust as Yahweh's highest representative.

For the inspired writers of the Old Testament, that was Moses' style of leadership, a style seldom transferred or attributed to others. Moses was the one leader remembered consistently as the servant of Yahweh (Josh 1:1–2, 7, 13–14; 8:31, 33; 9:24; 11:12, 15; 12:6; 13:8; 14:7; 18:7; 22:2, 4–5; compare 1 Kings 8:53, 56; 2 Kings 18:12; 21:8).

Even Israel's latest literature named Moses as Yahweh's servant (Neh 1:7–8; 2 Chron 1:3; 24:6; Mal 3:22). Moses was the esteemed servant without parallel. His leadership had freed Israel from slavery and established the nation. The Torah he gave led Israel throughout its history, no matter what its political status or organization. His Torah explained Israel's destruction and loss of national power. For Israel, to speak of the servant of

Yahweh was to speak of Moses. Prophets could be called "servant of Yahweh" (1 Kings 14:18; 2 Kings 17:13).

Kings, especially David, could be called God's servant (2 Sam 3:18; 7:8). Because of David, his servant, God promised to preserve his people and kingdom (1 Kings 11:13; 2 Kings 19:34). Because the people forgot the Torah of Moses, God's servant, David's political kingdom disappeared from history (2 Kings 21:8–15; compare 23:25–28). The prophet proclaimed hope for a new servant, a humble, suffering servant who would be a mediator for the people with God (Isa 53), imagery certainly pointing forward to Jesus of Nazareth, but imagery drawn partly from the history of Moses, the servant of Yahweh. The shadow of Moses thus extended beyond his death (Deut 34:5) over the nation's entire history.

The first Israelite leader to work in that shadow was Joshua. He shared with Moses the self-identity of slave of Yahweh, pleading for Yahweh's mercy (Josh 5:14). Such prayer came to characterize Israel's prayer tradition (Pss 86:2; 116:16; 123:2). However, never in his lifetime does the biblical record indicate that Joshua earned the respectful title, "servant of Yahweh." He constantly stood in the shadow of Moses, the servant of Yahweh, studying the Torah of Moses and fulfilling the commands and promises of Moses.

Finally, Joshua obtained the title, "servant of Yahweh"—at his death (Josh 24:29). In life he served as the minister of Moses. In death he became the servant of Yahweh. Thus he finally received that title one could not confer upon oneself except as a title of humility in prayer. The title was not basically a kingly title, used to exercise rule and authority over others, as it could easily become in a royal court. Rather, "servant of Yahweh" was a title conferred on a leader by the followers who recognized in the leader perfect obedience to Yahweh. For Israel, of course, perfect obedience to Yahweh meant perfect obedience to the Torah of Moses. God's first commission to Joshua concerned dedication to the Torah of Moses (1:7–9). That task, received at Moses' death, Joshua faithfully pursued and kept until his own death. Thus he became known as "servant of Yahweh."

A sad note appears at this point. Joshua willingly served in Moses' shadow. At Joshua's death the nation stepped out of that shadow. No one came forward to serve in the shadow of Joshua, much less in the shadow of Moses. Joshua left an impact on the people he led. "Israel served Yahweh all the days of Joshua and all the days of the elders who extended beyond Joshua's time and who knew all the work of Yahweh which he did for Israel" (24:31).

Joshua did not leave a new leader behind as had Moses. "And all that generation also were gathered to their fathers; and there arose another generation after them who did not know the Lord, nor yet the work He had done for Israel" (Judg 2:10 NASB). Disregard for the shadow of Moses dominated a whole era of Israel's history, an era summarized as "In those days there was no king in Israel; everyone did what was right in his own eyes (Judg 21:25 NASB). As leader, Joshua failed at one point. Leadership should produce leaders for the next generation. Joshua dedicated himself to the Torah of Moses but did not train someone else to do the same. Thus his leadership died out at his death.

At many points Joshua represented the supreme example of leadership in the shadow of Moses. He maintained an effective chain of command. He began by working through the national officials (1:10; 3:2). He concluded his ministry by summoning the officials at many levels of authority for final instructions and encouragement (Josh 23:2; compare 8:33). Joshua reminded them of God's history with them and then concluded a covenant with them (ch 24). He left behind elders who effectively led the people (24:31).

Joshua not only worked with the chain of command to communicate God's will to the people. He also cooperated with the priests God had set up to lead in the religious side of Israel's life. Joshua led the priests to assume prominent leadership roles at the Jordan miracle (chs 3–4) and in the conquest of Canaan (ch 6). Thus Joshua maintained the social order Moses had set up, giving the priests custody of the ark of the covenant. Joshua acknowledged other roles of the priests. Chief Priest Eleazar played a prominent role in allotting the land (14:1; 17:4; 19:51; 21:1). Thus his burial is noted as parallel to that of Joshua (24:33).

Joshua worked not only with his compatriot Eleazar but also with the younger Phinehas (22:13), letting the young priest settle the unity-threatening religious dispute with his own generation rather than taking matters in his own hands. Joshua thus knew how to share leadership with authorized religious officials.

He also knew how to share leadership with representatives of the people. He cooperated with the "heads of the fathers of the tribes of the sons of Israel" (14:1) in distributing the land. These are apparently the same people as the "chiefs" of 17:4. When a particular tribe had trouble, its leaders could readily approach Joshua and the other leaders, challenging Joshua and his chain of command to do what Moses had commanded (21:1). In a different approach, a leadership team from the tribes worked with the priest to prevent a split among the tribes (22:14, 21, 30–31). Joshua, then, did not perform as a one-man show. He studied Moses' Torah, used Moses' organization, and successfully led the people with the help of various levels of leadership among the people.

Leadership pointing to the past

Joshua tried to help future generations. He left memorials to teach them the way of Yahweh. Israel's landscapes lay strewn with items pointing the people of God to their past history with Yahweh. An Israelite tourist guide could easily follow Joshua's tracks, stopping to explain the lessons from Joshua's experiences with God. Parents had reason to remember Joshua as they took children to worship or on pilgrimage. Joshua had left behind a program to teach young children their nation's history with God. Israel had difficulty forgetting Joshua's story, which was actually God's story; for throughout the land lay markers of the past calling forth faith in the future. We can hear the tour leader now:

"Here at Gilgal we see twelve stones standing tall. They came from the River Jordan, where the faithful priests stood as they held the ark of the covenant high, marking the dry land God had created through the flooding Jordan. These stones call forth the praise of God from his people. He made it possible for us to cross the Jordan and have a homeland. The story of that crossing reminds us of another. Remember the other time God led his people through the currents? Of course, in similar fashion to the Jordan crossing, Israel had crossed the dry sea out of the land of Egypt, fleeing from slavery (Josh 4:9, 22–23). Israel has no excuse for forgetting God. These stones remind us; indeed, they call the whole earth to know 'the hand of Yahweh that it is strong in order that you may have respectful awe before Yahweh all the days' (2:24).

"Even the name of Israel's first camp in the promised land tells us a story. Here we stand on Gibeath-haaralotha, or as we say today, 'the hill of foreskins.' Joshua led Israel to identify themselves anew as the obedient people of God. He directed a ritual in which all eligible males were circumcised, a ritual Israel had neglected during the wilderness wanderings. This neglect, along with their slavery in Egypt, made Israel a reproach in God's eyes and in the eyes of their neighbors. Joshua, the man of Moses' Torah, rolled away that reproach. Thus he could call the first camp site—here at 'the hill of foreskins'—Gilgal, meaning 'rolled away' (5:9). This day we come to Gilgal and remember the God who rolls away our shame as we obediently serve him.

"Joshua's memorials point us to the bad times as well as the good," continues our guide. "Come with me to the Valley of Achor, or, more appropriately, the Valley of Aching (7:24). Look at this great pile of stones. It reminds us of Israel's aching, and especially of the aching of the family of Achan. You know the story. Achan refused to obey God's command. He took a robe and some gold and silver from the war loot after the victorious battle of Jericho. In so doing, he caused Israel to lose the first battle of Ai. God called on Joshua to exercise leadership in the realm of justice as well as in war. Through prayer and ritual Joshua followed God's instructions, found the guilty man, and led Israel to execute proper punishment. These memorial stones at Achor point us to obey God and avoid the ache of his punishment.

"Nearby, we see another heap of ruins. This is Ai, aptly named for our day, since Ai means, 'The Ruin.' Having resolved the case of Achan's aching, Joshua led Israel to capture and destroy Ai. The heap of ruins here shows us the reward God's people reap as they follow God's plans for life (8:28). A second heap stands here at Ai. It is a burial heap. Joshua sentenced the king of Ai to the humiliating death by hanging, then followed Moses' Torah (Deut 21:22–23) by removing the body at sunset and burying it. This heap of stones marks Ai's city gate and the final resting place for Ai's king, who dared oppose God and his people (8:29).

"Even as God's people go to worship, we find a memorial from Joshua. We notice servants drawing water from the wells and cutting wood to prepare for our sacrifices. These are the Gibeonites, who tricked Israel into signing a peace treaty. Joshua's leadership turned even a treacherous peace treaty with foreign enemies into an advantage for God's people. The trickery of Gibeon produced needed laborers for God's worship in the place God chose (9:27).

"Our tour of Israel takes us next to Makkedah," asserts our guide. "Here we see the famous cave. You cannot enter the cave, however. Joshua led the people to close up the cave's mouth with large stones, for the cave is the burial place for the five southern kings who formed a coalition against Joshua. Again, Joshua humiliated them, then followed Moses' Law in taking their bodies down from the tree and burying them in this cave before sunset (10:27). God's opponents cannot hide. No cave is too deep or dark for God and his people to discover its occupants. Look at the cave. Remember the power of God over any enemies who threaten you.

"Joshua's memorials do not always point us to the dead. Living memorials he left behind point us to the task that lies ahead. Joshua did not defeat all the people occupying the promised land. Some continue to live among us and threaten our existence (13:13; 15:63; 16:10). Peoples and land remain to be conquered before God's plan and our mission are accomplished.

"Joshua's leadership, like that of all mortals, had its limits. Old age (13:1; 23:1) caught up even with him. He had to leave part of the task to future generations (compare Judg 1:1–36; 2:1–5, 20–23; 3:1–4).

"Such generations had a role model to follow. Joshua was not the only faithful leader of his day. Caleb, his faithful cohort among Israel's original spies (Num 13:6), remained faithful and illustrated how to take the land assigned the tribes (Josh 14:6–15). Every time we go down to Hebron, we remember the faithful example of Caleb and the task that still remains (compare Judg 1:9–20).

"We need to turn our attention to one other place—Shechem. Here we find, perhaps, Joshua's most important memorials. Here stands an altar Joshua built. On its stones we see copies of Moses' Torah. We remember how Joshua taught Israel the Torah, calling both blessing and cursing upon them as Moses had taught (Josh 8:30–35; compare Deut 27). Joshua thus left us the practice of gathering all Israel together to hear God's Torah and to commit ourselves to that Torah. Joshua did more than that. At the end of his days he gathered us once more to Shechem and led us to commit ourselves to God's covenant. He wrote down our commitment in the Torah and set up a stone of witness. Every time we see the altar at Shechem and the memorial stone here, we recall our commitment. We cannot plead ignorance. We have pledged to obey God. When, instead, we deny him, then these memorials from Joshua witness against us and call us back to our commitment.

"This is a good note on which to conclude our tour of Joshua's memorials scattered for us over the promised land he led us to occupy. I hope you have learned the lesson of past memorials. Joshua's leadership and that of all good leaders is not limited to the problems of the present. Joshua, the good leader, looked forward and set up concrete memorials to let God's people remember many things, namely, what God had done; what happened to those who opposed God; the example of faithful heroes of the past; the task that remained unfinished; and the commitment to God and to his covenant that should never die."

[*Methodological note:* We have used the book's expression "until this day" to follow Joshua's leadership in establishing memorials. We have not exhausted every use of the expression, for the phrase does not always point to memorials present at the time of the author of the book of Joshua. On some occasions the expression "until this day" pointed to Joshua' day and realities which did not point to concrete memorials beyond that day. (See Joshua 22:3, 17; 23:8–9.)]

Leadership through action

Joshua stepped from the shadow of Moses to lead by example. Both God and the eastern tribes challenged him to action, action characterized by "conviction and courage" (1:6, 18). The remainder of the book shows that Joshua accepted the challenge. He showed conviction in his constant attention to Moses' Torah, in his handling the case of Achan's rebellion (ch 7), and in his final speech and covenant mediation.

Only a person of conviction could face Israel with such demands. Only a person of conviction could interpret Israel's past as a past of false gods, gods of the fathers beyond the river and in Egypt (24:15–16). Only a person of conviction could know the holy jealousy of God so well that he could bluntly tell Israel,

"You are not able to serve Yahweh, because a holy God is he, a jealous deity is he, one who will not forgive your sins and transgressions." (24:19)

Joshua strode forth in action because he had conviction about the nature of God and the history of his people. Only a person of such conviction can lead God's people. The next generation lost its convictions, dabbled a bit with each god they encountered, faced God's judgment, and looked for a leader with conviction to lead them back to their covenant commitment with God (book of Judges).

Joshua showed not only conviction but also courage in leading God's people. His courage enabled Joshua to risk looking foolish in order to carry out God's commission and guide the people into fulfillment of God's promises.

Courage called the east Jordan tribes to forsake the comfort of territory won and homes settled to show their loyalty and unity with the other tribes (chapter 1). Courage challenged purity-conscious priests to step into the flooding Jordan River carrying the precious Ark of the Covenant. Courage was required from grown men, faced with the need to endure circumcision to symbolize their commitment to God (chapter 5). Courage called the priests to circle a fortified enemy city daily, blowing trumpets against the world's oldest habitation and expecting the walls to fall (chapter 6).

Courage led people into battle. Courage demanded people divide the land according to God's lots rather than according to the strength and pressures individual tribes might exert. Courage allotted some of the best land to levitical priests to fulfill God's teaching (chapter 21). Leadership is going down God's path with conviction and courage. Such conviction and courage come because the leader knows God's presence, the presence that was with Moses (1:6, 18).

In summary, leadership normally includes planning: setting goals; determining strategy to achieve the goals; allotting resources in ways that will set priorities to achieve the goals. Here it appears that Joshua had a definite advantage. God had already set the goals. In most cases he determined the strategy for each action. He promised the necessary resources. On occasion, as with the battle strategy of Ai, Joshua set up some strategy, but more often God provided the battle plans. Joshua simply had to have the faith to execute God's plans.

Joshua's leadership operated in the shadow of Moses. It worked through tribal, national, and priestly organizations. It sought to leave memorials to provide leadership and courage for God's people far beyond Joshua's lifetime. Joshua's leadership worked to accomplish the tasks God had set out and to fulfill commands of the Torah of Moses. It unified the tribes in taking the land, distributing the land, and in committing themselves to God's covenant. But Joshua's leadership failed in one crucial point. It did not train leadership for the future, leadership which could maintain the unity of the people and continue the loyal commitment to God's covenant.

Still the verdict on Joshua is unanimous. He was great. God made him great (3:7), a greatness comparable only to the greatness of Moses (4:14). What one element characterized that greatness? People knew God was with Joshua as the Lord had been with Moses (3:7; compare 1:5; 6:27). Human greatness rests on divine presence. The greatest office a human can occupy is that of "servant of Yahweh."

2

THE LAND GOD GAVE

Leadership for Joshua had one focus: gaining the promised land for God's people. But what, in the book of Joshua, is significant about this land? It is land which must be conquered, possessed, and distributed. It is also land not possessed, land that remains. Before all this, it is land that has been promised, is being given, and should be inherited. It is land under God's holy ban. The topic of land thus reveals itself as a theme with complexity, a theme viewed within the book from different perspectives. To understand it in all its complexity, we must examine land from each of these perspectives.

Land as gift

Above all else in the book of Joshua, the land is a gift, "the land which I am giving to them, to the sons of Israel" (1:2). This can be stated both with a participle indicating present action (1:2) and with a Hebrew perfect tense indicating past action (1:3). Even before Israel crossed the Jordan, the land was theirs. God is giving and had given it to them. The gift is assured. No questions remained. No room for doubt was left.

Still, the gift did not come without action. Israel had to receive the gift. Israel had to follow God's instructions, cross the Jordan, and possess the land (1:11). God had not made an idealistic gift without roots in reality. God had made a gift; he expected it to have concrete form. He had a gift. He wanted his people to own and control that gift.

Israel, about to cross the Jordan, had reason to believe they could possess the gift. Part of Israel had already possessed their gift, their land (1:13–15). Land in Joshua thus has two parts—land possessed east of the Jordan and land to be possessed west of the Jordan. Both parts were God's gift to his people; both parts were the concern of all Israel. The part that had possessed the gift was not relieved of responsibility. That part must co-operate until all the land was possessed.

This land as gift was not just a theological ideal Israel had dreamed up. It was a reality the occupants of the land recognized (2:9). The gossip network worked in Canaan to let the peoples west of the Jordan know precisely what was happening east of the Jordan. For them it was obvious that ordinary human power could not have accomplished what Israel had accomplished.

Yahweh had acted in Egypt and beyond the Jordan. Now he was poised to act in Jericho. Who knew that better than a Canaanite prostitute who greeted Jericho's tourists? Rahab, the prostitute, knew how her people reacted to the news: courage disappeared, replaced by dread and fear (2:9, 11; compare 2:24; 5:1). They waited fearfully for Yahweh to cause Israel to possess what he had given.

Israel, too, knew Yahweh would let them possess the gift. Israel's representatives bargained with the prostitute on that basis (2:14) and testified to Joshua of God's gift, a testimony based on their experience with the faithful prostitute (2:24). They had more than that one experience on which to base their confidence in Yahweh's gift. Israel's history rested on the promise of the land to Abraham (Gen 12:7) and his descendants (Exod 6:4). Joshua's commission rested on that promise (Josh 1:6), but no generation could rest assured they would see the promise fulfilled. The rebellious wilderness generation had heard Yahweh swear they would not see the land (5:6).

Even Joshua's generation, commissioned to fulfill the promise, could not idly anticipate winning every city. Yahweh could give an unfaithful people into the hands of the enemy (7:7). Normally before each battle, Israel heard Yahweh's specific promise to give the enemy into Israel's hand (6:2, 16; 8:7, 18; 10:8, 19; 11:6). Typically, also, Yahweh gave each enemy into Israel's hands (20:30, 32; 11:8). So under Joshua's leadership, his generation of Israelites saw the promise to Abraham become reality (21:43). Israel had received the gift of the land.

The gift of the land theme thus displays part of its complexity. We must ask the question: When does God give the enemy and the land into Israel's hand, and when does he give Israel into the enemy's hand? Joshua phrased the question in a drastic form—"Alas, O Lord Yahweh, why have you so certainly caused this people to pass over the Jordan to give us into the hand of the Amorites to bring about our destruction? If only we had been content to live beyond Jordan" (7:7). Threat to the gift brings an even greater threat, one to the integrity of God; for if Israel's name is cut off from the earth, "then what will you do for your great name?" (7:9b).

Giving the land is thus more than simple military action with assured results. Giving the land is the way God chose to establish both his and his people's reputation in the world. Even such great stakes did not guarantee immediate success. God had shown patience in working and waiting with the wilderness generation. He was willing to show the same patience and make the same demands on the conquest generation. He could explain their defeat: "Israel has sinned. They have transgressed my covenant which I commanded them" (7:11).

Only a faithful covenant people could expect to receive the gift of the land. The history of promise never made the gift automatic for a particular generation. The gift continued to be reserved for a people of covenant, not for a people craving exotic goods and wealth.

The land as gift changed meaning at one specific moment in history. A promise became reality. A hope became a possession. A theological teaching became a personal testimony to a living experience. When this happened, the mode of communication also changed. Now one could say, "their inheritance which Moses had given to them beyond the Jordan eastward" (13:8), or they could refer to Joshua giving land to Caleb (14:13), and even to the sons of Israel giving land to Joshua (19:49–50). The gift of land could now be located in time, in space, and by human agency. Now the gift had concrete boundaries encompassing specific cities. Now one could know if the entire gift had been received or if more should be expected. One could know that "there remains a great amount of land to possess" (13:1) and could explicitly describe the boundaries of the remaining land (13:2–6).

Land as gift was not simply a mass of community property. The gift had specific recipients. Moses gave land to each tribe east of the Jordan "for their clans" (13:15, 24, 29). Land was not up for grabs to the strongest military leaders, the richest bidder, or the most clever political opportunist. Land was for each clan among God's people. Land was not a human property available to be awarded as prizes for service to the country and its leader. Land was God's gift to the families of his people to be used to support the family and to unite the tribe.

This becomes evident with the one tribe that did not participate in the gift of the land. Levi had been set aside for God's service (Num 18:20; Deut 18:1–2). No member of the tribe needed farm lands to work. They did need cities in which they could live among the people as they served God and his worship place. The Levites received no gift of land (Josh 13:14, 33; 14:3–4; 18:7). They received places to dwell with enough land for their cattle to graze (ch 21). Such cattle would provide food, clothing, and—especially—animals for sacrifice.

Levites lived in the cities. They did not exercise political control, nor did they own the sown land where farmers grew crops (21:12). Gift of land thus suited the needs of each of the tribes. This did not mean each tribe got all it wanted (17:14). It also did not mean all the land was given without human labor. Israel had to fight for its land. If the Joseph tribes wanted a larger gift, they had to fulfill God's commission to cut down the forests and prepare the land for agricultural use (17:15–18). Note that in clearing the land they faced strong opposition. They had to clear the land in faith that God would give it to them by defeating their enemies. Gift of land had to be received in faith that the God who promised was strong enough to deliver on his promises.

Gift fulfilled promise (21:43). It also symbolized threat. Gift was not guaranteed eternally. Israel could forfeit the gift. Trust in nations and their gods rather than trust in Yahweh threatened disaster. An unfaithful Israel would "wander away lost off this good land which Yahweh, your God, has given to you" (23:13b). The God who had proved faithful to his words of promise would also prove faithful to his words of threat (23:14–15). Faithless Israel faced destruction (23:15).

Yahweh remained sovereign even over His past promises and past actions. He controlled all land. He had given Mount Seir to Esau and the Edomites while letting his people go down and eventually endure slavery in Egypt (24:4). He could take the land he had given Israel and give it to someone else. Israel had not earned the land nor constructed its material improvements (24:13). The land as gift stood as symbol calling for faithful service to the Giver of the land (24:13–18). Land was tied to covenant. Land belonged to covenant people and only to covenant people. Otherwise, the people wandered off the land into Exile, waiting for God's next move without any grounds to command how, when, or if God would act. Only the future history of Israel and the future words and acts of God would determine if the gift of land would remain in Israel's hands.

Land as possession

Land as gift had to become land as possession. Joshua's first command to the people said, "Prepare provisions for yourselves, because within three days you (pl) will be crossing over this Jordan to enter in order to possess the land which Yahweh your God is giving you to possess it" (1:11).

Scholars have argued long and hard about a supposed basic meaning of the Hebrew term *yarash* (see WBC 7:17). Does Micah 6:15 prove its meaning is "to tread upon?" Do Genesis 15:3–4 and Jeremiah 49:1–2 show that "inherit" was the original emphasis? Or do the numerous appearances in Deuteronomy point to a technical military term? We may never know if a single meaning existed in the mind of any Hebrew speaker or what that meaning might have been. The word has developed a complexity of meaning beyond any simple English word and beyond any simple definition.

For our purposes, a traditional use can be shown to lie behind *yarash* in the book of Joshua. This use appears in the blessing Rebekah received from her family that her descendants would "possess the gate of those who hate them" (Gen 24:60). Study of Deuteronomy (2:12, 21–22, 24, 31; 4:47; 6:18) confirms this meaning; compare further Numbers 13:30; 21:24, 32, 35; 33:53. To "possess" includes "to dispossess." It involves taking land by force from someone who occupies the land. It means winning the right to transfer the title of the land from the defeated to the victor. In other contexts, *yarash* may mean something else, but in the context of conquest in Numbers, Deuteronomy, and Joshua, *yarash* means "dispossess and take over."

This is the way God chose to complete the link between promise to patriarch (Gen 15:7) and life in the land (Josh 1:11; compare Gen 22:17; 28:4; Num 33:53; Deut 1:8, 21, 39; 3:12, 18, 20; 31:3). God's gift of land thus involved human participation in battle. In Joshua 3:10 Joshua could use a form of *yarash* to say Israel's God would "drive out" or "dispossess" the long list of peoples then inhabiting the land. "Dispossession" was God's activity as well as Israel's. (Compare 8:7.)

Possession of land involved all Israel. Moses gave the tribes east of the Jordan possession of their land. That did not complete their participation in land possession activities. They, too, had to cross the Jordan armed for battle to help the tribes west of the Jordan gain possession of their land (1:14–15). Tribes having won their land were not free to exercise possession of that land until all the tribes could exercise land possession rights (22:4, 9; Hebrew *achuzzah*). God did not intend Israel to be a loosely related collection of fiercely independent tribes. He called the tribes of Israel to gain their identity as part of the one people of God, each acting on behalf of the other.

Israel's God even provided an option for his people east of the Jordan. If they thought their land was ritually impure because the chosen worship place was not in their territory, then they could move west of the Jordan. God would provide a possession for them there. Trying to set up worship in opposition to Yahweh's way was not the answer. Trusting him to provide them a possession in the "land of the possession of Yahweh" was (22:19; Hebrew *achuzzah*).

After their series of military actions, Israel had destroyed the many city state kings of the land and possessed their land both east (12:1, 6) and west (12:7) of the Jordan. God had fulfilled his promise (11:23), but still "there remains a great amount of land to possess" (13:1). Possession of the land was not only a past event. It was also a future goal. Joshua's advanced age interrupted the parade of possession. So did the tribes' failure or inability to dispossess some of the native inhabitants (13:13; 15:63; 16:10; 17:12–13; compare 19:47).

This left the rest of the task to another generation, but the next generation did not fulfill the task. They could not blame Yahweh. He had "dispossessed" the nations (23:9; compare 21:43). He stopped only when Israel stuck with the nations rather than with Yahweh (23:8, 12–13). The blame lay with

Israel. They lacked the committed leadership to accomplish the task. Only with David did the proper leadership in Moses' shadow come forth to complete the task. Still, the divine promise stood: "I will dispossess them before the sons of Israel" (13:6; compare 23:5). The example of Joshua's generation also stood. As Caleb phrased it, "If, however, Yahweh be with me, then I will dispossess them, just as Yahweh spoke" (14:12; compare 15:14). Joshua's challenge to his generation called succeeding generations to action: "How long will you prove yourselves to be lazy cowards in regard to entering to possess the land which Yahweh, the God of your fathers, has given you?" (18:3).

Land as inheritance

Yahweh gave Israel the land to possess as an inheritance from him. The image created here is significant. An inheritance passes to a new generation at the death of the patriarch. God was the father passing his inheritance on to his sons. This inheritance proves unique. The Father did not die, nor did the sons get sovereign, everlasting control of the inheritance. Here we see the limits of human language used to symbolize and communicate truths about the reality of human relationships with God. God the Father wanted to share with his children from his "estate." He willingly gave them the land he controlled. He let them control his property. Why? Because He had promised the patriarchal fathers he would give them the inheritance (1:6). Right to possess an inherited homeland belonged to Israel by virtue of divine oath sworn to a previous generation, not by virtue of land laws they could enforce in human society. Israel's inheritance remained an inheritance Yahweh had to give, one they had to (dis)possess.

Interestingly, the term *inheritance* or *homeland* (Hebrew, *nachalah*) does not appear in the first half of the body of the book (chs 2–12). Rather, it becomes important only after the conquest is complete and the distribution of the land begins. God

42

commanded Joshua to distribute the land as an inheritance, even the uncontrolled, unconquered land that remained (13:6). The tribes east of the Jordan had their inheritance from Moses (13:8). The service of God in making sacrifices for him constituted the Levites' inheritance (13:14, 33). No territory, only cities and pastures, formed their inheritance (ch 21). Joshua's task was to define the inheritance of the nine and a half tribes (13:7). He accomplished this in chapters 14–19, with the help of Eleazar and his lot (14:1–2). Caleb's inheritance was unique, sworn to him "forever" because "you remained totally loyal to Yahweh, my God" (14:9).

Inheritance was tied so closely to the clan or family that daughters received inheritance to protect family claims when no sons were available to claim the inheritance (17:4–6). The inheritance involved concrete boundaries that could be surveyed and written up (18:4). The ultimate action for Joshua was to let the people go, each clan to its inheritance (24:28). *Gift* pointed back to the promise God made to the patriarchs. *Possession* pointed to present ownership wrested from previous inhabitants. *Inheritance* pointed to claims for the future. No government or private action seeking to assure ownership of the clan's possession would ever be valid, for inheritance rights came from God, not from human agencies. (Compare 1 Kings 21:3.)

Land by lot

Divine inheritance easily left room for human manipulation. A tribe could claim its territory was too small (17:14). Or a tribal territory might be too large (19:9). Past promises had to be fulfilled (14:9), and each family's claims had to be considered (17:3–6). How could humans make decisions with divine authority? How could they avoid the dangers of human manipulation? God had the answer. Joshua did not make decisions alone. He had a selected commission with representatives from each tribe survey the land and divide it into appropriate portions. Then he relied upon Eleazar the priest to symbolize God's presence in the activity.

The decision itself as to which tribe got which territory became quite "mechanical." The lot decided. This followed God's instructions through Moses (Num 26:52–56; 33:54). The lots were apparently stone objects used to gain impartial decisions, decisions usually interpreted as coming from God (Prov 16:33). Casting lots was often connected with the high priest (Lev 16:8), but pagan sailors also cast lots (Jon 1:7). We would expect Eleazar to be present to cast the lots for Joshua. Such expectations appear to be confirmed, since the lots were cast in Shiloh at the tent of meeting (18:1; 19:51). Still, the text surprises us. Usually no actor is named. Again, we would surmise that the passive constructions favor divine action by the divine representative—the priest. One text names the thrower of the lots: "Joshua threw the lots for them in Shiloh before Yahweh" (18:10; compare v 6).

Israel did not have to fear human manipulation of land claims as the tribes received their inheritances. Human manipulation disappeared because "mechanical" lots were used to show God's will as Moses commanded and because Joshua, the great, respected leader in Moses' shadow, threw the lots. The lot fell for each tribe and for each of the Levitical families. The mysterious lot had faithfully determined Israel's property claims once and for all. The lots' results stood written in Joshua's records. New inheritance claims came only within a clan or family. The family's claims had been allotted. No room for human manipulation remained. Faithful Joshua had carried out the commands God gave Moses. Israel could not ask for anything more.

Land under the ban

Holy war[9] is the major theme of the book of Joshua if one listens to most theological discussions of the book. Indeed, the systematic theologian may want to reflect on the function and meaning of the image of God, the Warrior, in the book of Joshua and elsewhere in Scripture. The theologian may seek to describe the adequacy of that image of God in light of the Bible's emphasis on the Suffering Servant, the Good Shepherd, the Prince of Peace, and the crucified Messiah. In so doing the theologian must deal honestly with the structure and contents of Joshua.

The book of Joshua does not explain the nature or reason for war. It does not reflect upon the image of God, the Warrior. Joshua assumes war as a human activity; indeed, as *the* human activity by which territory changes hands among nations. Joshua joins the members of its environment in assuming that divine power and authority is revealed through human wars. For the book of Joshua, the question never comes down to, "Would God fight?" or "Why would God fight?" or "Is it moral to speak of God participating in the bloodshed of war?"

The book of Joshua focuses on God's promise to the fathers. He bound himself to give his people the land. To give them the land, other people had to lose the land. Deuteronomy used this situation to warn Israel against human pride, explaining that the gift of the land did not reflect Israel's righteousness. It reflected the occupying nations' wickedness (Deut 9:4–6; compare Lev 18:24–25, 27–28; Deut 18:12).

Judges explained the remaining nations as needed to teach untrained generations of Israelites the art of warfare (3:1–2). Joshua does not explain why the nations lost the land. It simply underlines God's positive note. God promised to give the land. He did give the land. Israel possessed and inherited the land.

For Joshua, the question is how a land occupied by strong enemies with ancient claims can be transferred to a young, upstart nation without experience or power. Joshua's answer is quite simple. Israel possessed the land through the ban (Hebrew *cherem*). The ban represented God's way of doing war to protect Israel from the temptation to worship other gods (Deut 7:1–4). The same treatment awaited an Israelite city which fell to the seduction of foreign gods (Deut 18:12-17). The ban was not Israel's normal procedure in warfare. Normally, Israel would offer a city the opportunity to surrender peacefully (Deut 20:10). A rebellious city faced the ban, but then only the males stood under the ban (Deut 20:13-14). The total ban was God's special warfare technique on the cities of the promised land to preserve the infant nation's religious fidelity (Deut 20:16-18).

The book of Joshua presumes the deuteronomic regulations for conquest and Deuteronomy's stories of Moses applying the ban east of the Jordon (Josh 2:10; compare Deut 2:34; 3:6). Joshua centers attention on how Israel reacted to God's way of war. They could be self-seeking, wanting human glory rather than glory for God. They could be greedy, wanting war's booty for themselves rather than giving it to God. They could be sly and conniving, pretending to follow God's instructions but doing so only halfway. The ban tested Israel's faithfulness. How would they react?

Jericho presented the first test (6:18). Would covetousness prove Israel's downfall, so that "you would then set up the camp of Israel for the ban" (6:18)? Can banning Israel be banned? Apparently not. "They set everything in the city under the ban, male and female, young and old, cattle, sheep, and donkey were devoted to the sword" (6:21). "The city they burned with fire and everything which was in it. Only the silver and the gold and the utensils of bronze and iron they gave to the treasury house of Yahweh" (6:24).

Alas! That was not the whole story. "The sons of Israel disregarded the ban. Achan . . . took part of the banned goods. Then the anger of Yahweh burned against the sons of Israel" (7:1). An Israel polluted by sin became overconfident, deciding its own strategy for battle (7:3). They met defeat. Why? "Israel has sinned. They have transgressed my covenant which I commanded them. They have taken from the banned goods, stolen, deceived, and put them among their own things. Unable to stand before their enemies, the sons of Israel turn their backs to their enemies, because they have become banned goods. Never again will I be with you if you do not banish the banned goods from your midst" (7:11–12).

The ban represented God's covenant. Breaking the ban broke Israel's covenant relationship with God. It transferred Israel from being God's people to being God's banned goods, from victors to vanquished, from sanctified to sinners. Refusal to carry out the ban was theft and deception.

God took the ban seriously, so seriously that only capital punishment could remove Israel from God's list of banned goods (7:15). Israel learned the dramatic lesson. They put Ai to the ban (8:26). Here, however, exceptions were made, "according to the word of Yahweh, which he commanded Joshua" (8:27). Rules for the ban were not absolute. God's direct command could modify ban laws as he chose. The ban was not an inflexible system of an inflexible God. It was a divine test to determine the loyalty of a people as well as a divine method to deliver an uncontaminated gift of land to his people. It was also a method which cost the inhabitants of the land their confidence, bringing fear to their heads (2:10; 10:1–2).

Thus Yahweh's method became Joshua's method (10:28, 35, 37, 39). "Everything that breathed he put to the ban just as Yahweh, the God of Israel, commanded" (10:40; compare 11:12, 21). The obedient Joshua found that God made his task easier. "For it had been Yahweh's idea to harden their hearts to encounter Israel in battle in order that they could put them to the ban without their having opportunity to plead for mercy. Indeed, this was so that they might annihilate them just as Yahweh commanded Moses" (11:20).

What then is the message of the ban for the book of Joshua?

To protect Israel against the major sin of idolatry, God commanded her not to show mercy to the enemy. To enable her to keep the commandment, God caused her enemies to fight her rather than seek mercy and peace. (WBC 7:130)

The Land God Gave   47

To forsake the ban was to forsake Yahweh. Israel did that once (7:1). It brought a lesson Israel never forgot (22:20).

Israel possessed God's gift of land because God placed that land under the ban and because Israel under Joshua obediently carried out the ban. Ideally, Israel should have had the perfect situation—possession of a land with no one left to tempt them to forsake Yahweh. The ideal did not match reality. Reality described what remained: "a great amount of land to possess" (13:1). That meant a great number of foreign people with a great number of foreign gods giving Israel a great number of temptations. Israel faced the future with a great challenge. They faced it with the experience of God's ban, a ban which proved God's power to give Israel the land. They faced the challenge with God's promise to deliver that land to them. Seldom again would they put an enemy under the ban. Why? Because seldom again would they have a leader like Joshua. Instead, they had impatient leaders like Saul (1 Sam 15). Wars of conquest gradually turned to wars of defense against invaders, wars in which the laws of ban did not apply. God remained active in Israel's battles on and off the battlefield, and God's inspired spokesmen, looking to the future, prophesied continued protection of and a prosperous future for his people. Such language underlined God's active involvement in all aspects of the life of his people against any temptation to see God as a passive observer of human life. Such language also declared God's deliverance from trials and tribulations where only divine activity could explain such deliverance. Finally, such language testified to the sovereignty of God over every type of opponent which might claim power that belonged only to the one God. The ban meant no power could oppose Yahweh and emerge victorious.

The land of rest

The ban was an intermediate word for Israel. It provided a means for an end. It was not the goal. The goal for Israel in the book of Joshua was rest (1:13, 15). "Rest" says little to the English-speaking world, but for the Hebrew-speaking world, *nuach* brought great meaning. Rest was the spiritual and physical condition of the person God delivered from trouble (Ps 116:7).

One of life's great complaints was that I "have found no rest" (Jer 45:3 NASB). The Temple was God's "resting place" (Ps 132:8 NASB). Rest was the needed change of routine from daily labor (Exod 20:12; Deut 5:14). The king's word could be "comforting" (2 Sam 14:17 NASB, with a form of the Hebrew *nuach*). "To rest" was to stand still and firm as did the feet of the priests in the Jordan River (Josh 3:13) or as did the stones set firmly in the ground (4:38).

God's goal for Moses and the Israelites in the wilderness was to give them rest (Exod 33:14), a theme repeated in Deuteronomy (3:20; 12:9–10; 25:19). Rest was a national goal, not a tribal or individual one. No tribe or group of tribes was to enjoy rest "until Yahweh gives rest to your brothers just as to you" (Josh 1:15). After helping the Israelites capture Jericho, Rahab and her clan received their reward—rest outside but near the camp of Israel (6:23). In 11:23 Israel had "rest" from war, but that represents another Hebrew word (*shoqtah*), emphasizing still, quiet, silent, inactivity (compare 14:15; Judg 3:11; 5:31; 8:28; Ps 83:1).

"Rest" (*nuach*) means more. "Rest" was the fulfillment of God's promise to the fathers with no enemies to threaten them (Josh 21:44). What God promised Moses (Exod 33:14) and the East Jordan tribes (1:13–15; 22:4), he brought to pass in history. Rest is not a theoretical, spiritual state enjoyed by individuals; it is a "state of the union" the nation enjoys. Rest is a lasting state (23:1) measured in months and years.

Rest offers God's people a choice. They may choose to reject God's rest (see Isa 28:12). Thus Joshua concluded his ministry among Israel with a final sermon (ch 23) and a covenant ceremony (ch 24) calling on Israel to accept God's rest by obeying His word. But Israel refused to listen. Rest was lost and regained as an intermittent possession (Judges).

Finally, David led the nation to enjoy anew God's rest (2 Sam 7:1, 9–11). That prepared the way for God's promise to "establish the throne of his (Solomon's) kingdom forever" (2 Sam 7:13 NASB; compare 1 Kings 8:56). But that did not solve the problem. The future was not secure. Moses had already painted the picture of a dreary future for a disobedient people: "the Lord will scatter you among all peoples. . . . and among those nations you shall find no rest (*targia*), and there shall be no resting place (*manoach*) for the sole of your foot" (Deut 28:65 NASB).

> Rest can be a reality for Israel. It can be a goal lost and looked forward to again. It can even be a goal regained. Whatever stage Israel finds herself in, rest is a term with a concrete content. It represents freedom from enemy oppression and deadly war. It represents life lived with God by the gift of God. . . . Rest, not war, is the ultimate goal of Israel. . . . But . . . rest could be won only through war (WBC 7:22).

Thus, rest for God's people in God's land comes through God's ban.

This is the theme of land in Joshua. Land is a distinct geographical location (1:4, chs 13–21) as well as a promise to the fathers, a gift from God, a possession for a specific generation of people, an inheritance pointing to long-term possession through the generations. Land does not come into possession through magical means. Land is claimed by other people. God's people must wage war under God's conditions to gain possession of the gift. But continuing war is not the goal. The ban is not the eternal practice. Even possession of the land is not the final purpose for the book of Joshua. The theme of land possession points to rest. God prepared land for his people in order to prepare them for His kind of life, the life of rest.

3

THE LAW THAT LEADS GOD'S PEOPLE

God's people could possess God's gift of land and enjoy rest because God had given them the way that leads to rest. That way is *law* or to use the more far-reaching Hebrew term—*Torah*.[10] Torah ordinarily meant instruction, particularly instruction one received from a priest on religious questions (Jer 18:18; Ezek 7:26; Hos 4:6; Hag 2:11–13). In like manner, Isaiah's teaching was Torah for his followers (Isa 8:16). Wise men produced Torah (Prov 13:14), a practice with roots stretching back into Israelite family life (Prov 1:8; 4:4, 11). Above all, Torah was instruction God gave his people for obedient living in commitment to him (Gen 26:5). Israel was supposed to do everything possible to remember and testify to God's Torah (Exod 13:9). God tested to see if they would be faithful to keep Torah (Exod 16:4), but Israel could not pass the test (Exod 16:28).

Torah defined

Torah referred, then, to teaching, particularly God's teaching, received in several forms. Some forms of Torah came

51

through oral teaching. That instruction might be passed on by word of mouth for generations. Some Torah might be written down. Normally, however, when Israel heard the word "Torah," it signified one thing: the Torah of Moses. Moses' chief task had been to teach Israel God's way (Exod 18:20). His teaching soon appeared in written form. Some was written on stone tablets (Exod 24:12) and some in the book of the covenant which Moses read to Israel (Exod 24:7). Ultimately, Moses' Torah became a large book filled with the teachings God had given his people through Moses (Deut 28:58; 30:10; 31:24), a book stored by the ark of the covenant in the worship place (Deut 31:26). As such it warned God's people of the curses they could bring down on themselves, but it also served as a constant guide to the leader of God's people:

> when he (the king Yahweh chooses) sits on the throne of his kingdom, he shall write for himself a copy of this law (Torah) on a scroll in the presence of the Levitical priests. And it shall be with him, and he shall read it all the days of his life, that he may learn to fear the Lord his God, by carefully observing all the words of this law and these statutes, that his heart may not be lifted up above his countrymen (literally brothers) and that he may not turn aside from the commandment, to the right or the left, in order that he and his sons may continue long in his kingdom in the midst of Israel. (Deut 17:18–20 NASB)

Joshua's call to obey Torah

Yahweh did not choose a king in Joshua's generation. Instead, he installed Joshua as the prime example of a leader in the shadow of Moses. God's commissioning speech to Joshua centered in faithfulness to Torah: "Just have great conviction and courage to obey carefully the whole Torah which Moses, my servant, commanded you. Do not turn away from it to the right nor to the left so that you may prudently prosper everywhere you go. This book of the Torah shall not depart from your lips. You shall meditate upon it day and night in order that you may obey carefully according to everything which is written in it, because then you shall make your paths successful, and then you will be prudently prosperous" (Josh 1:7–8)

Torah, in the book of Joshua, is first of all the leader's leader. Torah programmed Joshua for success and wisdom. A leader in Joshua's position would expect to spend time recruiting and training an army, gathering public support, and studying military strategy. God had another path for Joshua. He called Joshua to solitary study of Moses' Law. Why? God did not need a leader with such natural ability and military genius that he could win by his own wits. Such a leader would simply become proud and self-confident, ignoring God and his way of life.

Solomon and Rehoboam served later as prime examples of this. God's plan for a leader was to avoid all opportunity for pride (Deut 17:20). God wanted a leader to know God's role in the people's military history, God's call to covenant obedience, and God's promise to be present and lead to victory, giving Israel the land. Only extended experience with God's Torah could produce that type of person. Torah obedience was not a lifestyle that rulers imposed on the lower classes. Torah obedience was a lifestyle that leaders modeled before the people they led. Torah obedience was the only path to success (compare 2 Kings 17:37; 22–23).

The call to Torah obedience placed the leader in an awkward position. He was not the principal lawmaker for his people. He was a law-taker. He did not stand in a position to claim new revelation from God, revelation which updated or superseded previous revelation. The basic rules for the life of the people as individuals and as a people stood ready at hand for each generation of Israelite leaders after Moses. New insights concerning life with God and continuing historical acts of God might find their way into inspired writings (Prophets and Writings), but such writings still only supplemented the irreplaceable Torah. From first to last in the nation's history, leader and people searched Torah to know God's will. They knew Torah was the criterion for judgment in their lives before God. The leader had many functions, but all other duties became subservient to the daily duty to study and follow Torah. "Only he who obeyed Moses the leader of Israel could expect success in his leadership endeavors" (WBC 7:19). Joshua set the example for all of Israel's leaders after Joshua. In the midst of the campaigns of conquest, he led the people to the place God chose—Shechem. There he built the altar as God commanded through the Torah of Moses (8:30–31). He copied the Torah for the people to see (8:32). He carried out the covenant ceremony as Moses commanded. He read the Torah to the people, reading every word (8:33–35).

Torah was not a secret book the leader could use to control and dominate the people. The people did not have to wait for the leader's good pleasure to know God's teaching. God commanded that the leader teach the people. Obediently, Joshua did so. Torah obedience became public priority number one for every person dwelling in Israel. This meant no class of people in Israel had a monopoly on God's will. Nothing gave one person closer access to God than another. Social class, education, gender, citizenship, family roots, clan history—none of these at times imposing qualifications—singled out one person for closer relationship to God than another. "Women and children, and the aliens active among them" (8:35) had rights and responsibilities to hear and heed God's Torah.

Torah as community responsibility

Knowing Torah, moreover, was not a contest at which one person took pride in excelling over another. Keeping Torah was both an individual and a corporate function. When one person disobeyed Torah, the entire community suffered (Josh 7). The sin of one person brought the entire community to Shechem to renew covenant and rehearse Torah (8:30–35). Each individual had responsibility before God and before the community to keep Torah. The community as a whole and as a group of individuals had responsibility to see that no one transgressed the Torah. The community which dealt properly with transgression and renewed covenant commitment to Torah could expect to hear the leader bless the people as Moses commanded (8:33). Thus, they could regain their identity as covenant people of God. "With the law of Moses and the leadership of Joshua, Israel could again pass over into the covenant, be the people of God, and enjoy the blessings of God" (WBC 7:95).

Torah and daily life

Torah gave direction to all of life. Since Torah was so important for Israel's leaders and in Israel's public ceremonies, one could easily conclude that Torah directed public life, that is, political and worship life, but that daily life on the farm or in the village required a different kind of direction. The temptation lay near to turn to the model of the original inhabitants of the land for direction. Such a model centered on the cult of Baal and its promise of fertility for family, flocks, and fields. Joshua showed such a model had no claim in Israel. He sent the East Jordan tribes back across the river with one command ringing in their ears, "Only, be exceedingly careful to obey the commandments and the Torah, which Moses, the servant of Yahweh, commanded you, to love Yahweh, your God, and to walk in all his ways and to obey his commandments and to cleave to him and to serve him with all your heart and with all your being" (Josh 22:5).

Torah obedience as love

Here we learn the nature of Torah. Torah is more than an objective set of rules forced on an unwilling, or at best, neutral people. Torah obedience is not a human effort to win God's favor and thus to ensure personal security with God and perpetual safety in the land. Long before Jesus summarized the commandments in terms of love (Matt 22:34–40), Joshua summoned the East Jordan tribes to Torah obedience, an obedience best illustrated in love of God (Josh 23:11). Love of God is more than an emotional attachment. Love of God is a moral attachment, an attachment so intense that one commits oneself to obey God's Torah without question. Such obedience does not transform the free human creation into a moral robot. Such obedience stems from trusting love so deep that it knows the Beloved would never have moral expectations that led to less than the best for the people loved. Torah obedience "is the definition of the people of God. The human-God relationship is not a legalism done in fear, nor a business transaction done with pride of achievement. It is a love and devotion relationship, obeying and worshiping out of free choice" (WBC 7:245).

Torah and disobedience

Torah allows no excuses for disobedience. The people returning to their land in rest heard Joshua set before them the same demand God had originally set before him (23:6; compare 1:7). Such a demand did not come in ideal circumstances. God, through Joshua, sent the people out to live in the land while remnants of the nations still lived among them (23:7). Torah obedience should come despite the strongest of temptations. Foreign worship and alien gods would constantly lure Israel to follow them and forsake Yahweh. Torah would constantly call Israel back to Yahweh. Trust in the God of Torah should always prove stronger than the call of false gods and false worship, but such trust was not easy. Such trust required "great courage" (23:6). The book of Joshua left Israel with the haunting question, Did Israel have the strength and courage required to follow Torah rather than succumb to the lure of Baal and the other gods native to the land?

Torah as covenant keeping

Torah obedience is covenant keeping, for the words of covenant are written in the book of Torah (24:26). The covenant relationship is the Torah relationship, a relationship requiring courage, love, devotion, and total commitment. To make covenant words on a par with Torah words is to modify the definition of Torah. The ending of the book of Joshua implies that Torah of Moses is not God's only Torah. "Joshua wrote these words in the book of the Torah of God" (24:26). The Torah of Moses stood tall in the commanding position over all Israel's history, but God had further instructions for His covenant people. Such words may consciously advocate adding the book of Joshua to Torah of Moses, leading to Israel's larger canon of Scripture. Such words called Israel to remain faithful to Torah of Moses while at the same time listening to the words of faithful leaders who called them to covenant obedience. The covenant words, explaining and calling for obedience to Torah of Moses, could also be written into the Torah of God.

Torah was not the only writing preserving the word of God. The "book of the upright" (Josh 10:13) preserved words that became part of Scripture (compare 1 Samuel 1:18 and the early Greek translation of 1 Kings 8:12–13). God worked in many ways to preserve his word, even using writings that eventually faded from history. Such writings proved to be God's intermediate step on the way from proclamation of word in history to preservation of word in the Bible. (Compare Joshua 18:9, a border description which may lie behind the following chapters of Joshua.)

The Word of Yahweh

Torah is not the only vocabulary item used for authoritative directions from God. The book of Joshua also points to the spoken word of God. Different Hebrew vocabulary items are used to talk about oral word of God. Both the noun formulation, "word of God," and the verbal formulation, "Yahweh said," are used.

Word of God and written Torah

Hebrew root vocabulary items *dabar* and *'amar* appear with little distinction in meaning. The verbs communicate Israel's belief that God's word came in direct oral form as well as in the written form of the Torah of Moses. God spoke to Joshua directly, giving directions, for example, for Joshua's leadership and Israel's actions (1:1–9). Such oral speech by God sent Joshua back to Moses' Torah. The implication here is that Israel knew God speaking in two ways: oral and written. The two ways were complementary, not contradictory. One manner of speaking pointed the listener to the other. New oral revelation did not try to replace traditional written revelation. Rather, the oral word of God reinforced his written word.

Such reinforcement could include interpretation for a specific situation. God told Joshua the specific regulations for the ban on Ai (8:27) though Moses had already taught the general regulations (Deut 20:16–18; compare Josh 11:6, 9). At other times Joshua carried out Moses' command totally (Josh 10:40; 11:12). As situations changed, God brought a new word giving directions for the new situation. God gave Joshua explicit instructions to carry out the conquest of the entire land with explicit descriptions of the land's boundaries (1:1–4). Joshua became old, and much work remained unfinished (13:1). God recognized Joshua's age, personal needs, and limits. He issued another word that turned Joshua from conquest to land distribution (13:1–7). Again this oral word was related to the Torah of Moses, simply showing when to carry out the original word Moses received (14:5).

Functions of word of God

God's word was not limited to one mode or one function of speech. He did not always face Israel and Joshua with commands in the imperative mode. He also addressed encouraging words to

Joshua (3:7). Such words gave Joshua a motivation to carry out God's commands. These words pointed to a sign of divine presence in Joshua's actions with Israel. Word of God thus functioned both to give his people directions and to lead them to follow those directions. Such encouraging, directing words followed Israel step by step through the land (6:2–5; 8:1, 18; 10:8; 11:6).

Chapter 3 shows another facet of the word of God. Joshua served as mediator of God's word. God spoke to Joshua, and Joshua relayed the message to the people. The people recognized what God was doing and followed Joshua's commands, knowing they came from God (compare 4:8).

Addition of the Hebrew word *tsiwwah* to our vocabulary items for word of God leads another step forward here: "But the priests who carry the ark were standing in the middle of the Jordan until everything was complete which Yahweh commanded Joshua to speak to the people according to all which Moses commanded Joshua" (4:10).

Careful reading of chapters 3 and 4 shows that God directed each step Joshua and the people took in crossing the Jordan. This direction came in the form of oral word of God to Joshua. This is summarized in 4:8: "The sons of Israel acted just as Joshua had commanded. They carried twelve stones from the middle of the Jordan just as Yahweh had spoken to Joshua." We are tempted to ask, "How does Moses fit into this picture?" This calls us to a closer look. The summary in 4:10 reaches back further than to 3:1 It marks the conclusion to all that began in chapter 1 and relates specifically to 1:3, then on back to Deuteronomy 11:22–25; 32:44–47. God promised Moses an obedient Israel would conquer the land. He told Moses to lead the people to the edge of the land and prepare the people to cross the Jordan into the promised land under Joshua. Joshua 4:10 shows that Israel was God's obedient people, ready to receive God's promises to Moses. Action of the moment might feature conversation between God and Joshua for the people; ultimately, however, even word of God to Joshua fulfilled word of God to Moses (compare Josh 20:1–2). Torah formed the foundation for all of God's conversation with his people. The entire conquest followed the plan God gave Moses to give to Joshua (11:15, 23).

God's conversation with Joshua filled still another function for Joshua. It interpreted what God was doing for his people at the present moment. God not only commanded Joshua to circumcise the people (ch 5). He also interpreted the meaning of that particular circumcision rite. Through the circumcision, God "rolled the disgrace of Israel away from you" (5:9). Israel was not simply an obedient people ready for conquest. They were a purified people no longer tainted by the social disgrace of slavery in Egypt nor by the cultic disgrace of uncircumcision in the wilderness. Israel became aware of their freedom from disgrace and thus their renewed freedom to serve God because God spoke to Joshua.

As often in the early Old Testament narratives, God's word did not always come directly from Yahweh. At times it came from a messenger seen as a man (Josh 5:13–15; compare Gen 18). The messenger revealed to Joshua the holy nature of the place where they met, at the same time connecting Joshua to Moses and his call to service through the same speech pattern (Exod 3:5).

God's oral word for Israel could become a word of judgment for a sinful people (Josh 7:10–13). The word of judgment served not simply to supply information and condemn. It became a word of guidance, leading Israel to the way to restore the covenant relationship. Restoration of covenant relationship demanded drastic action, in Israel's case in Joshua 7, capital punishment for the guilty family. This word of judgment thus shows how serious God takes his demands for obedience. When his people took his word with the same seriousness, they became a restored people. A restored people could again hear God's word of encouragement and direction to take the land (8:1).

God's word for any one situation was not automatic and predictable. God expected his people to inquire after his word (9:14). When they did not, they found themselves acting against God's will. Again, God directed them through the situation, but only after a serious breach of God's directions and a dispute among the people threatened to divide God's people. Moses and Joshua could not claim a monopoly on God's word. God also spoke to the Levites (13:14, 33; compare Num 18:20; Deut 10:9; 18:2). The Levites, however, had to go to Joshua to ensure he carried out God's word to them (Josh 21:2).

Joshua was also not the only person who knew the word of God as given to Moses. Caleb remembered God's promise to him and his clan through Moses. He acted on this word, asking Joshua to fulfill it (14:6; 15:13; compare Numbers 14:24; Deuteronomy 1:36). Joshua and God honored such forthright faith (Josh 14:13). Women could act in similar fashion, asking the rights Moses gave them be recognized (Josh 17:4; compare Numbers 27:1–11). They had obeyed Moses (Num 36:1–12) and claimed their land rights from Joshua.

The book of Joshua reminds us of one other important element of God's word. God could communicate to his people without words. He gave to them the mysterious device know as the lot. With this they could determine his will for distributing the land. Lots were apparently stone objects used to gain impartial decisions. The people saw them as more than just impartial decision-givers. They saw the lots as mediators of God's decision, thus God's silent word (see Joshua 14:2; 15:1; 16:1; 17:1; 21:4). The lot was probably used in identifying Achan as the culprit in Joshua 7. Using the lot, Israel learned what "Yahweh commanded by the hand of Moses by lot" (21:8).

The faithful word

God's word could be commanding, directing, encouraging, judging, or simply communicating information. It could come through Moses, through Joshua, through a messenger, to Levites, or to Caleb. It could be spoken, written, or even silent. It could apply to men, to women, to priests, or to the nation. One thing remained the same. God was faithful to his word. "Not a single word fell from every good word which Yahweh spoke to the house of Israel. Everything came to pass" (21:45). Whatever situation Israel found itself in, one constant remained. She could not blame God. "God had faithfully done for Israel what he promised. Blame belonged on Israel's shoulders, not God's" (WBC 7:235). Thus "the faithful community of God reads history as the story of God's directing promises" (WBC 7:236).

Past history with God's word means one can trust that word for the future. Trust in that word runs in two directions. God will bring the blessings He promises (23:5), but people of God must also remember, "it will be the case that just as every good word which Yahweh, your God, spoke to you has come upon you, just so Yahweh will bring upon you every evil word until he has destroyed you from upon this good land which Yahweh, your God, has given to you" (23:15). The good word of promise is not a static object which creates an eternal condition. God's word is a dynamic reality, going forth in written and oral forms to his people, calling to covenant obedience. It changes a people without land to a conquering nation controlling all the land. Equally, it can change a disobedient nation in charge of its destiny to a slave people carried off their land in utter defeat. God's word remains in control of history, calling forth a faithful people to study Torah (23:6), follow him, and see his good words come to pass. Such a Torah-studying people cannot pay attention only to good words with promises of blessing; they must listen equally as carefully to the evil word with its threat of judgment and curse. Both are the authoritative word of the one God. That word points us to look back and see what God has done (24:2–13) so that we can look at the present to see that word's demand on us (24:14–24) and can look to the future to know how he will respond to us as he continues to act in the history of his people (ch 23).

4

LOYALTY THAT CHARACTERIZES GOD'S PEOPLE

The book of Joshua identifies one major characteristic that separates the people of God from all other people. Yahweh's people have no other gods. They are absolutely loyal to Yahweh. Modern Christians see nothing unusual here. Loyalty to the one God is the only option they know. Many today could not even name another god. A large percentage have no personal acquaintance with people who worship another god. In our culture the only options have traditionally been: to worship or not to worship. Then we choose our denomination and fight the other ones.

Loyalty as unique to Israel

Israel's culture was quite different. Everyone worshiped someone. Everyone but Israel worshiped more than one someone. The quest was not loyal devotion to one god to the exclusion of others. The quest was loyalty to a personal god while not offending the other gods who controlled the many different arenas of life. Religiously, one had to cover all bases. In such a world, Yahweh distinguished himself among the gods. He called for absolute devotion to himself and rejection of anyone else. He was all or nothing at all. His call separated him from all other religious practice. To worship Yahweh meant to break the rules of Near Eastern religious custom. It meant to snub other peoples and their religious traditions. It meant to deny the religious practices which objective observation might claim to have worked adequately through the long centuries in the land of Palestine. To worship Yahweh, to obey Torah, meant to be odd, different from all the other peoples of the world.

Loyalty in community

The East Jordan tribes represent one side of this identity of loyalty. They represent community loyalty, loyalty to the people of God. Israel learned community in the tedious classroom of history. Their tradition gave them few examples of loyalty. Isaac and Ishmael, Jacob and Esau, Joseph and his brothers—all modelled self-interest, jealousy, separation, rivalry, and even hatred. Only in their brief better moments did unity and community shine forth. After Joshua, the period of the Judges would feature brief cooperative actions separated by long periods of isolation. Tribal jealousy and even tribal annihilation marked this period for Israel. Next Saul and David struggled for leadership. Then David faced opposition from his own sons. Solomon's united reign led to the dissatisfaction of the northern tribes and their decision to follow Jeroboam rather than Solomon's son Rehoboam.

Separation continued through the end of the kingdoms and into the Exile. Exile thrust Israel's people into all parts of the world. The Diaspora became a continuing reality. Return from Exile introduced other divisions—people from Exile and people who had faithfully cared for the homeland; people who returned faithfully to the land and people who chose to stay behind in Babylon; people in the land and the diaspora scattered over the earth. Gradually, the split between Jews and Samaritans emerged and deepened.

Finally, sects such as the Essenes gave vivid life to the different theological viewpoints within the one people of God. The rise of the Christian church brought a split that appeared to be final.

Through all this, the book of Joshua offered an example of the community loyalty God expected and of how to deal with threats to that loyalty. The example centered in the East Jordan tribes—Reuben, Gad, and the half-tribe of Manasseh. They had no personal reason to appear in the activities of the book of Joshua. They had conquered their land. Moses had given them their tribal inheritances. God had given them rest. They were ready to settle down and enjoy life in the land. But Joshua quickly interrupted such plans. Pointing them to God's word through Moses, Joshua called the East Jordan tribes to arms in support of their West Jordan kin (Josh 1:12–15). No one tribe was to enjoy possession of its inheritance until all the tribes could find rest in their inheritances. The East Jordan answer serves as a model for all the people of God: "Everything which you have commanded us, we will do; everywhere you send us, we will go" (1:16).

Community loyalty places personal desire under the command of God's chosen leader. The leader whose actions reflect God's presence gains the absolute obedience of the people. They are willing to promise, "Every man who rebels against your order and does not obey your words to the last detail which you command us shall be put to death" (1:18). The East Jordan tribes had learned the meaning of being part of the people of God. Israel was not a loosely organized group, joining together only in crisis situations. Israel was not just a people with similar worship patterns joining for occasional national worship services. Israel was a unified body. Threat to Israel did not lie in geographical differences. It lay in the threat to lose their sense of loyalty. No matter where people lived or what their personal economic situation, Israel had to remain one body dedicated to one land. The call for Israel to act went out to all Israel, not a part of Israel. When any one part did not possess its inherited land in rest, no part of Israel could rest. Rest and land possession came to all at once. Thus the East Jordan armies left their houses and families to cross the Jordan in march of conquest (4:12).

The movement goes in the other direction. When the book of Joshua lists Israel's accomplishments in conquering the land, it begins not with the accomplishments listed in Joshua. It begins with the accomplishments of the East Jordan tribes (12:1–6). Every care is taken to emphasize the work of all Israel. No group can laud itself over other groups within God's people. When God's people function properly, all can point to the part they played. Together under God they conquered the land, inheritance enough for all the tribes of Israel.

Similarly, before land is apportioned to the West Jordan tribes, the inherited land of the East Jordan tribes is listed (13:1–33). To list Israel's land is to list the land of twelve tribes, not just that of those Joshua led west of the Jordan. Even when the land distribution action simply shifts locations, the point is renewed that the East Jordan tribes are part of Israel and have allotments given by Moses (18:7).

East Jordan tribes were not forgotten when Israel set up cities of refuge (20:8) nor when Israel established cities for the Levites (21:7, 36–39). The action of the book may center in conquest and distribution of West Jordan, but the theme of the book is the community loyalty of all twelve tribes. A subpoint here is the tribe of Levi. The cultic tribe of priestly helpers did not expect a tribal allotment. Still, the allotments repeatedly include Levi among the tribes and explain why Levi did not have an allotment (13:14, 33; 18:7). A concluding act of land allotment is to give cities where the Levites can live and carry out their responsibilities even though they do not have an official territory. These cities of the Levites form another joining element in Israel, for the cities come from each of the tribes (ch 21). East Jordan tribes may be separated from the main body of Israel geographically by the Jordan River. Levites may be separated sociologically by their cultic function and by their status as not owning land and not forming a political subgroup. Both remain solid parts of the community of Israel. Israel cannot be described without describing East Jordan tribes and Levites. Community loyalty is an overarching characteristic of Israel.

The East Jordan tribes and community loyalty take center stage in chapter 22. They kept their word spoken in chapter 1 (1:12–15; 22:1–4). They joined all Israel in having obligation to obey the Torah (22:5). They received Joshua's blessing (22:6–8) and could possess their land (22:9). There they faced the problem: isolation. How did a people separated geographically maintain their community loyalty? Their answer: build an altar of witness to remind them of the religious and historical ties that bound them to their people west of the Jordan.

This created a greater problem. Had the search for community loyalty violated the command of Torah obedience? Tribes of West Jordan thought so. Moses allowed no other altars except where Yahweh chose. A separate altar meant separate worship. The altar could not be a sign of community loyalty. It represented community division. Worse, it represented apostasy from Yahweh. It represented a refusal to learn the lesson of history, history which occurred east of the Jordan in Peor (Num 25). It represented a threat to the entire community of God's people. The West Jordan tribes did not react in jealousy or with a view to their own superiority. They had a solution, one that involved sacrifice on their part. They were willing to share their inherited land with the East Jordan tribes to preserve community loyalty and to prevent divine wrath (22:19–20).

Such drastic action was unnecessary. East Jordan tribes had acted to preserve community loyalty, not disrupt it; to maintain loyalty to Yahweh, not to rebel against him. They were looking to the future and protecting themselves against future dangers, against being forgotten or unwanted among the community called Israel. They wanted a witness all could use to remember the ties between east and west. The one thing which joined east and west was the common witness to Yahweh as the one God. This was the social and religious cement which held community loyalty together. "Cult and geography could separate. Proclamation of Yahweh as the present God unified" (WBC, 7:250).

Loyalty as individual devotion

Community loyalty was matched by individual loyalty. In the book of Joshua, Caleb stands out as the supreme example of individual loyalty.

> "I was forty years old when Moses, the servant of Yahweh, sent me from Kadesh Barnea to spy out the land. I returned the word to him just as it was on my heart. My brothers who went up with me caused the heart of the people to melt, but I remained totally loyal to Yahweh, my God." (14:7–8)

Caleb carried out the task God sent him on and brought back the report God expected. He let neither human fear nor crowd frenzy detour him from the faith. He was loyal to his community and to his God. He received his reward (14:14). Such individual loyalty lay at the root of all that was Israel. Only with individuals expressing full commitment to Yahweh and his will could Israel hope for community loyalty. In the book of Joshua and through much of the Old Testament, individual loyalty seems to take a back seat to community loyalty. The example of Caleb reminds us of the strong role of individuals in forming the community covenant loyalty that stands as the backbone of Israel's identity.

Loyalty as covenant commitment

Individual and community loyalty find their concrete expression in the covenant. God made covenants with two individuals before He made the covenant with the nation. Both individual covenants had results reaching far beyond the individual. With Noah, God promised that a flood would never again destroy the earth and its life (Gen 9:11, 15). With Abraham, God established the covenant of circumcision, promising to make Abraham the father of a great nation and to give that nation a land to live in (Gen 17:1–14).

God remembered his covenant with Abraham and acted in the Exodus to fulfill that covenant (Exod 2:24; 6:4–5). Through Moses, God established his covenant with the people Israel in the wilderness at the holy mountain. This covenant Israel was called to keep. Through it God would make Israel a holy nation, a kingdom of priests, a personal possession (Exod 19:5–6). This was a covenant of obedience based on experience of God's saving power.

The people of Israel freely committed themselves to obey covenant law and be people of Yahweh (Exod 19:8; 24:3). The covenant regulations became a book Moses could read to the people, eliciting the people's renewed commitment to keep the covenant (Exod 24:7–8). This is the foundation for the book of Deuteronomy which sees the Ten Commandments as the center of the covenant (Deut 4:13). The teachings of Deuteronomy reflect the covenant God made or renewed with the people in Moab, reinforcing the covenant made at the holy mountain (Deut 29:1). It is a covenant for future generations (Deut 29:14–15) and has two possible responses: obedience or rebellion, with corresponding results: blessing or curse (Deut 27–28). The basis of covenant was the Law or Torah Moses wrote and placed beside the ark of the covenant (Deut 31:9, 25–26).

The word *covenant* is a relatively rare word in the book of Joshua except for the formulaic name of the symbol of God's presence—the ark of the covenant. The reality of covenant dominates the entire book. Having crossed the Jordan, Israel delayed conquest activities until the people had "rolled away" their social disgrace of slavery in Egypt and their national disgrace of not keeping the covenant of Abraham through circumcision. They ate the Passover meal, remembering the Exodus and wilderness experiences and the covenant commitment which went with those experiences (Josh 5). The first battle resulted in breaking God's covenant and facing the consequences (7:11, 15). For the first time, Israel learned in practical historical event rather than in the more theoretical sermons of Moses what breaking God's covenant brought. The punishment of Achan and his family impressed upon Israel the sovereign seriousness of God in his expectations of his people and of his commitment to his threatened curses as well as to his promised blessings. Covenant was not an interesting game one played spasmodically with God.

Covenant was:
- a relationship one constantly maintained;
- a relationship initiated by God;
- a relationship based on God's saving actions;
- a relationship desired by the people because of the love and power God had displayed for them;
- a relationship demanding loyal obedience to the Torah from the people;
- a relationship to which the people had freely committed themselves;
- a relationship which did not stand permanent and certain no matter how the people acted; but
- a relationship which must be daily kept or formally renewed.

Joshua interrupted battle plans to take his people to the place God had chosen—Shechem—and there renew God's covenant with his people (8:30–35). Such covenant renewal returned to the basis of the covenant—God's Torah. Joshua used every means possible to impress upon the people the contents of Torah. He wrote it. He read it. He gave the blessings and the curses. He let every person hear every word. Only with the serious nature of covenant fresh in their memories could Israel proceed with its plans for conquest. Conquest belonged to a covenant people, not to a greedy people.

Soon, however, Israel compromised covenant. Israel did not investigate the situation closely enough and made a covenant with the Gibeonites. This covenant came when Israel did not inquire of Yahweh (9:14). This covenant explicitly violated the Torah of Moses and the Covenant of Yahweh (Deut 7:2). Joshua saved the day for Israel. He brought Gibeon under the curse (Josh 9:23), rather than Israel, and made Gibeon subservient to Israel. Rather than separating Israel from her covenant with God, the incident came to make Gibeonites an essential part of Israel's preparations for worship of God. Having so narrowly missed covenant disaster, Israel could conclude the conquest. In fact, the covenant with the Gibeonites became the rallying point for the next enemies Israel would meet (Josh 10:1).

The importance of covenant for the book of Joshua becomes evident in chapters 23 and 24. The climactic chapters of the book turn to covenant forms and covenant language to identify the nature of God's people and show the goal of conquest. Chapter 23 reminds Israel of covenant threat:

> "When you transgress the covenant of Yahweh, your God, that he commanded you, and you go off and serve other gods and bow down in worship to them, then the anger of Yahweh will burn against you and you will quickly wander away, lost from this good land which he has given to you." (23:16)

Covenant threat means breaking of relationship with God in favor of other gods. It means refusing to love God (23:11). It means not obeying Torah. It means loss of land. It means forfeiture of divine gift. It means curse rather than blessing. It means

rest is not the final word for people in the land. Blessing will last only as long as total faithfulness to Yahweh lasts.

When Israel begins to experiment with other gods, trying to be like the nations and worship every god possible, doom is imminent. Doom means loss of the promised and given land. Doom means aimless wandering, searching for a home like the ancient patriarchal father. Doom means destruction, death, disintegration of the people of God. (WBC 7:257)

Doom is not the final word. Renewal is. Chapter 24 shows how a people under threat can come to God's place of worship and renew the covenant. Covenant renewal means memory of what God has done in the past. It means recognition of who God is. It means free commitment to Yahweh in full knowledge of his jealousy and of his total commitment to the blessings and curses of the covenant. It means risking commitment to the impossible.

Human logic leads people away from covenant renewal. Logic says covenant renewal is the option of desperation or hallucination. Covenant renewal appears to be human promise without chance of fulfillment. Covenant renewal appears to be guaranteed breaking of the covenant and thus guaranteed punishment from God. Covenant renewal appears to be an invitation to God to bring on the covenant curses.

Still, Israel enters the covenant. Why? "Far be it from us, the forsaking of Yahweh to serve other gods, for Yahweh is our God. He is the one who brought us up and our fathers from the land of Egypt, from the house of service, and who did before our eyes these great signs. He protected us in all the way in which we went and among all the peoples through whose midst we passed. Yahweh drove out all the peoples, indeed the Amorite living in the land, from before us. Yes, we will also serve Yahweh, because he is our God." Israel enters the covenant anew not because of something Israel can do to keep the covenant. Israel enters the covenant because she knows what Yahweh has done and can do. Yahweh has provided all the necessary evidence. His acts in history have shown he and he alone is Israel's God.

Israel thus found themselves without any options. Only one God proved great enough to serve. Only one God proved to deserve their loyalty. Only one God fulfilled the conditions to be God. Yahweh had proved to be the only God. Israel knew their limitations. They could not serve God. They must meet God with their failures. Still, they had no other place to turn.

The compelling evidence of national and personal history with Yahweh provided all the reason necessary to pledge loyalty to him in covenant renewal. In such renewal Israel confessed that God's covenant expectations were fair and were good for their lives. Israel confessed that they should follow God's way of life. Israel chose loyalty to God as the path they wanted to take.

Covenant thus defined loyalty for Israel. Covenant meant one people served one God by obeying one Torah in all situations. Covenant loyalty thus joined individuals and tribes into the covenant community. Covenant loyalty marked Israel off from all other peoples as the one people loyal to only one God for all areas of life. Covenant loyalty identified Israel as the people of the Lord of history.

5

THE LORD BEHIND HISTORY

Joshua is the star of the book of Joshua, commanding center stage throughout the book. The hero, however, is Yahweh, the living Lord of Israel and Israel's history.[12] Joshua calls others to action. He gives commands. He receives credit for victories. He becomes great. Joshua is involved in all the action, but Yahweh remains sovereign. Often, he gives opening directions and then apparently disappears from the action to let Joshua occupy the stage of history; but ultimately and actually, Yahweh has initiated and concluded the action. He has caused events to turn out the way they did. Final praise goes to Yahweh, not to Joshua. Joshua may appear to have the limelight, but Yahweh stands behind the decisive acts. He is the hero.

The central topic of the book of Joshua is thus Yahweh, the God of Israel; but how does one describe Yahweh? The book takes little time in offering adjectives or titles to describe God. Often it assumes readers already understand the basic nature of God. In fact, it assumes that the reader knows the promises to the patriarchs and the acts of the Exodus. The reader is expected to know the name of God—Yahweh—and its meaning

(Exod 3: 6). The reader is expected to know Joshua's previous preparation for leadership under God (Deut 1:37–38; 3:21–22, 28; 31:2–8, 14–15, 23). One is expected to understand the covenant relationship God initiated (Exod 19–24; 34). The reader can retell the religious history of Abraham and Jacob beyond the river with other gods. The book of Joshua does not try to introduce Yahweh to Israel or to the readers of the book. The writer, instead, tries to reemphasize with new examples what the reader should already know but can so easily forget. In many ways, the book of Joshua is a review of the topic of Yahweh, the God of Israel. The inspired author leads readers to remember that God speaks, acts in history, demands, faithfully fulfills his word, gives, is angry and jealous, and is present with his people.

God who speaks

The opening and basic statement of the book of Joshua about God is a simple one: God speaks. The Old Testament knows nothing of an absentee landlord God or an impersonal Creator who leaves and ignores his creation. The God of the Old Testament, and especially of the book of Joshua, is the God who consistently maintains contact with his people, giving his word to direct their life. We reviewed much of the evidence at this point in looking at the Torah or Law of God as it was expressed in the word of God. Here we need to reflect upon the meaning of God's speaking for our consideration of the nature of God himself. To say that God speaks to his people is to say that God is personal. God enters into conversation with his people. He does not treat his people as puppets or robots. He respects their freedom, outlining his plans for them and letting them choose to follow his plans or those of their own conceiving. He does this in every area of their life. He calls a leader (1:1–9). He encourages the leader (3:7–8). He guides them in establishing ways to communicate their history and their faith to future generations (4:1–3). He directs the actions of the people in their history (4:15–16), but not when the people do not ask for direction (9:14). He establishes rituals to ensure the people are in right relationship with God (5:2, 9). He sanctifies the leader of the people, preparing him for the tasks ahead (5:15). He gives instructions for battle (6:2–5; 8:1–2; 10:8; 11:6). He condemns a sinful people but shows them how to deal with their sinfulness (7:10–15). He recognizes the physical condition of his aged leader and adjusts plans accordingly (13:1–7). He sets up cities of refuge, establishing a system of justice for inadvertent killings (20:1–6). He recites his history with his people to encourage a new generation to follow him and renew the covenant with him (24:2–13).

God's direct speech drives the book of Joshua forward, affecting battle, ritual, and legal systems, as well as the direct personal relationship between God and people. Life of the people of God thus depends upon the spoken word of God. If God does not speak, God's people are without direction in every area of life.

Speech of God is something more than past event recorded in community memory or in written Torah. As we have seen above in discussing the Law of God, word of God delivered in the past plays a dynamic and central role in the book of Joshua. God's people do not survive simply on those authoritative words from the past. They need something more. They need words which give direction to new situations arising in the present. People of God live in this dynamic interaction between words from the past and words for the present.

Words from the past remain authoritative. They must be fulfilled. They may be promises to the fathers still to be fulfilled, commands from the past governing the covenant relationship as the command to love (22:5), promises to individuals or groups which the people must recognize and fulfill (14:6–14; 17:36), or threats for the future (23:15–16). Each word from the past has meaning for the present. Such words from the past do not cover all situations. God's people need more. They need the word of the present to thrust God's people into action on his mission for today. They need to know who God's choice for present leadership is. They need to receive encouragement for leader and people facing tough choices. They need conviction of present sin and assurance that forgiveness is available. They need direction away from current actions when new situations and conditions call for a change of plans. They need a call to covenant renewal. They need a new understanding of the serious bond the covenant forms between God and people.

In a sense, the people of the book always need more than the canon of Scripture. They also need the personal witness of the God who speaks, directing them to the book and directing into the arena of modern life with its demands and situations. They need to know how under current conditions

> "to obey the commandments and the Torah, which Moses, the servant of Yahweh, commanded you, to love Yahweh, your God, and to walk in all his ways and to obey his commandments and to cleave to him and to serve him with all your heart and with all your being." (22:5)

God's people can find out how to do this because Yahweh, the God of Israel, is a God who spoke in the past and who continues to speak in the present day. The God who gave his Word still gives his word.

Modern readers of the book of Joshua ask one further question: How did (does) God speak to his people? Here the book of Joshua offers little assistance. It simply assumes that God speaks, that his people understand his word, and that his people face the decision to obey or not to obey that word. Normally, the "how" question is ignored.

In chapter 5 the mysterious figure of the "prince of the host of Yahweh" represents God to Joshua. In determining the tribal territories, the more objective "lot" is used. Otherwise, language of normal human conversation appears. God speaks like a person to a person, usually Joshua. The Bible thus does not give a "canonical" method by which God must speak to his people. Rather, the Bible leaves the freedom for God to speak as he chooses. The Bible assumes that God's people can hear his voice and respond to it. Thus, conversation between God and his people can occur as portrayed in Joshua 7:6–15.

The biblical question is not how God speaks nor how people hear. The biblical question is: Do people listen and respond? The book of Joshua joins the entire biblical canon in calling people to expect God to speak and in challenging them to follow the message they receive. A major aspect of God's nature is his ability to speak like a person. The God of the Bible is the God who has spoken and who continues to speak.

God who acts in history

The God of Joshua puts actions to his words. He tells Joshua what to do and then provides the promised results. The narrative generally describes the activities of Joshua and the people. They cross the river. They carry stones. They set up ambushes. They march around walls. They discover kings in caves. They spy out land. They announce boundaries. They listen to Joshua speak. The overwhelming majority of action verbs in the book have Joshua or the people as subjects.

Divine acts and human acts

The concluding and transition sentences most often feature Yahweh as subject. The people have acted. Yahweh has brought the results. Joshua's introductory summary in 1:11 displays this theme:

"Prepare provisions for yourselves, because within three days you will be crossing over this Jordan to enter in order to possess the land which Yahweh your God is giving you to possess it."

Israel must prepare provisions. Israel must cross the Jordan. Israel must enter the land and possess it. All along, however, Yahweh gives the land. This is the nature of Yahweh, the God of Israel. He acts in the history of his people, but he acts alongside of and through the actions of his people. Yahweh is not the lone champion like a Goliath, marching out alone to challenge the enemy by himself. Instead, God is the leader of a people. He plots the course of action. He speaks with his people and communicates his plan. They accept the plan and move out in action. As they do, they find God fulfills his promise, prepares their way, and lets them accomplish their purpose even against overwhelming odds. The action of God is normally accompanied by action of his people, action he has called them to take.

Responses to divine acts

God acts in different ways to fulfill his purposes in history. The book of Joshua illustrates some of these. He uses the gossip systems of the enemy people to frighten them and prepare them for defeat (2:8–11; compare 9:9–11; 10:1–2; 11:1). Such gossip systems even teach lessons about the nature of God himself. It caused Rahab to confess, "Yahweh your God it is who is God in heaven above and upon the earth below" (2:11; compare Deut 4:39; 1 Kgs 8:23).

Other nations often confessed that their gods had led them into battle and brought victory. Most nations had specific gods of war who were expected to lead their armies to victory.

Such gods of war might or might not be the high, national god. Such gods could face challenges from other gods. Wars in heaven could ensue. A god or a group of gods could challenge the heavenly regime and come away victorious. The god leading a nation's armies might face serious challenges in the heavenly realm. Victory as god on earth did not secure the god's claim as eternal ruler of the heavens. The reverse case was also true. Claim as the national god ruling the heavens did not set a god up for eternal security. The god's fortunes often depended upon the nation's fortunes in battle. Thus, the major gods of Egypt took differing roles in the heavenly realms as the different dynasties came and went. The gods of Babylon took new forms and identities as historical fortunes changed or as the whims of kings gave loyalty to one rather than the other.

Israel's god was different. Yahweh was the God of heaven and earth. Earthly fortunes might lead people, particularly enemies, to confess or not confess Yahweh's unique nature. Yahweh's great acts in Egypt and east of the Jordan could activate the gossip chain and terrify the inhabitants of Canaan. His acts in history testified to his eternal power and dominion. They could lead people to recognize God's nature. Such acts did not change Yahweh's nature or increase his realm. He was Lord of heaven and earth by nature, not by historical act. He had no need to fear that another god could rob him of territory or limit his rule in heaven through earthly acts. Yahweh had no competition, in reality. No other god existed who could compete with him. Historical acts only gave evidence of eternal reality. God was the only God in heaven and on earth.

Through the story of Rahab, Israel confessed this eternal nature of Yahweh. Sadly, Israel could not learn the lesson for long. Yahweh's acts were not the only reality in Israel's history. Israel's refusal to learn the lesson of those acts was the parallel reality.

Israel kept searching for other gods on earth who could complement and supplement the acts of Yahweh. They wanted to compartmentalize Yahweh into the god of war or the god of politics. They were quite generous with other gods, offering them places beside Yahweh in the Temple and in the local high places. They gladly let the foreign gods take over responsibility for fertility or for protection of the family or for protection of the dead. Israel suffered through a long, torturous history of idolatry because they would not learn the lessons of God's acts in history, a lesson that Rahab, the Canaanite prostitute, readily learned.

Israel did learn enough of the history lesson to proceed with the conquest. The spies came back to Joshua from Jericho with a far different report than the spies brought back to Moses from Hebron: "They told Joshua that Yahweh had given into our hand the whole land. All the inhabitants of the land even melt before us" (Josh 2:24; contrast Num 13:25–33). God had used reports of Canaanite gossip channels to help convince Israel what it should have learned in the Exodus. Yahweh had no peers. He alone was Lord of heaven and earth.

Divine acts as wonders

The acts of Yahweh were not simply normal historical events for which Israel gave credit to Yahweh. The acts were far beyond what people normally expect in history. Yahweh could work with the priests in the ark of the covenant "in order that you may know the way which you are to follow, since you have never passed over in the way" (Josh 3:4).

Israel looked for more. They looked to Yahweh to "perform wonders among you" (3:5). This Hebrew word (niphla᾿oth) is not a major vocabulary item in the book of Joshua. In fact, it occurs only the one time. Where it occurs is important. It introduces the entire conquest narrative. It becomes the subject heading for all that is to follow. Every act of conquest is one of the "wonders" of God. No matter how intensely Israel works to fight the enemy, the final result is a divine "wonder." A wonder describes human reaction to events totally unexpected in the human realm. They are unusual, impossible, miraculous. Such events astound human observers. They lead the human witness to recognize human limitations and to praise God for his greatness and power. Thus, wonders belong to the language of praise and appear in the great majority of cases in biblical psalms. Wonders are God's historical actions which far exceed all human expectations.

In this sense, wonders are not necessarily the breaking of "natural laws." Rather, they are the exceeding of human imagination. Wonders are God's acts delivering his people or his worshiper from an impossible historical situation. In the book of Joshua, the "wonders" center on the crossing of the Jordan in parallel to the crossing of the Red Sea done "on the morrow" (3:5); but wonders are not limited to that one event. The morrow extends through the entire conquest event. What Yahweh did to give Israel the land was Yahweh's wonders for Israel. The ability to cross the river and take the land did not come from normal human capabilities. Such ability came only because Yahweh was working in Israel's history on their behalf.

The living God

Such wonders had two results. They drove out the native inhabitants of the land and proved the presence of the "living God" (3:10; compare Hos 2:1; Pss 18:47; 42:3; 84:3; Deut 5:23; 1 Sam 17:26; 2 Kgs 19:4, 26; Jer 10:10; 23:26; Dan 6:21). This title, like that of the God of heaven and earth, gains meaning only in contrast to the other gods of Israel's environment. Such gods depended on their worshipers for life. They had to be created by the worshiper from gold, silver, and wood. They had to be painted or plated, and fed, and carried in procession. They had to be placed on the divine throne in their temples. Israel could easily see Yahweh in the same light. In fact, Israel often wanted to.

Israel wanted to build bull images to represent God's presence. They were tempted to look upon the ark of the covenant as the throne upon which God sat and which they could carry in processions to represent his presence. They desired to see their sacrifices as necessary to God's well-being. They tended to confine God to his house in their Temple. They sometimes succumbed to the idolatrous notion of creating Yahweh in the image of Baal. God and his inspired writers would not let Israel do that without warning. Yahweh was not like the gods of the nations. Yahweh was different. He had a life of his own apart from the actions and buildings of his people. Yahweh was distinctive. He was the one and only "living God."

> Only Yahweh is active and alive. Only Yahweh intervenes in the affairs of His people. God's actions for his people prove his power and demonstrate the nature of his person. (WBC 7:46–47)

This became most clear in the conquest. Yahweh had no Temple, nor had Israel built any image to represent him. The ark of the covenant represented his presence but offered nothing visible to prove that presence. God had to act in Israel's history to prove his presence as the only living God. By leading his people across the Jordan and by giving them victory over their enemies and possession of enemy territory, Yahweh proved his vitality, power, and life. He had life in and of himself without any creative action on the part of his people. He was the source of their life, not the result of their living actions.

The God whose presence Israel saw symbolized in the ark of the covenant was the only "living God." Thus he and he alone was "Lord of all the earth" (3:11, 13; compare Mic 4:13; Zech 4:14; 6:5; Ps 97:5; 114:7). This title carried multiple meaning for Israel because the Hebrew term for "earth" carried multiple meanings. It could mean "land." As such it pointed to Yahweh as the God of the land of Canaan. The gods of the people inhabiting the land before Israel claimed to be god of the land. They made false claims. Before Israel set foot on the land, Yahweh was god of all the land. Canaanite gods faced their limits. They were the gods of the people who worshiped them. They were the gods of Canaan. They could call themselves "god of the earth," but that earth had severe limits.

Yahweh appeared to many to be in the same category. He had to fight to get land, and then could claim to be God only of the land he conquered. Israel knew differently. Yahweh faced no territorial limits. "Land" meant more than the land of Canaan. It meant the entire earth. It included all kingdoms and all kings. Yahweh was God of the land and of the whole earth no matter how great or small the kingdom his people ruled at the moment. Israel's loss of territory or status did not affect Yahweh's realm. The one who rode the ark of the covenant was "Lord of all the earth."

This theological theme gave Israel hope throughout her existence. Israel could rule the kingdom of David and Solomon, or Israel could languish in exile in Babylon. This did not affect the power of Yahweh. He remained the Lord of all the earth with ability and authority to act once more in history to give Israel the land and establish the people anew. History depended on Yahweh's purposes and plans, not on one nation's military fortunes.

Divine acts and worship

God's acts in history thus provided meaning for the titles Israel used to describe God. God's acts also gave content to Israel's worship and teaching. Parents could use the memorials Israel left scattered over the land to teach children the lessons of history. Such lessons did not center on human heroes or on dates and places. Such lessons centered on what Yahweh had done for his people (4:6–7, 20–24). The lessons of history had a much wider audience than children in view. The memorial stones were set up at Gilgal, Israel's early worship center. There Israel came to worship. There Israel observed Passover (5:10).

The memorial stones taught Israel at worship the reason for worship. They worshiped the God who had given them the land, the God who dried up the Red Sea and the Jordan River to establish his people in the land promised to the fathers. Such knowledge should lead Israel to worship and to "have respectful awe before Yahweh all the days" (4:24). The stones' audience extended beyond Israel and their worship. They testified "so that all the peoples of the earth might know the hand of Yahweh that it is strong" (4:24).

This focus on witness to the nations is a natural complement to the titles of Yahweh. If he is the only living God, the Lord of heaven and earth, the Lord of all the earth, then he is the only reasonable object of worship for all the peoples of the earth. Israel cannot expect jealously to protect a monopoly on Yahweh. Israel must expect the actions to witness to Rahab and her Canaanite friends. Israel must expect Yahweh's acts in history to call forth praise from all peoples, not just Israel. All too often, however, Israel sought alone to worship Yahweh while joining the nations in the worship of their gods. Israel answered the call of Baal and Ashteroth, of Marduk and Ashur to come and worship. Israel failed to call all the peoples of the earth to know the hand of Yahweh. The actions behind the book of Joshua and the writing of the book were done for Israel's benefit. Israel should have learned the lessons of history. She should have seen that God's plan involved the nations as well as Israel.

Israel should have understood that the God of all the earth had purposes far beyond one nation. Israel remembered the promise to the fathers that Israel would gain the land. Israel conveniently ignored the call to the patriarchs to provide blessing for the nations. God's historical acts provided the evidence that God had power over the nations. They also provided Israel evidence of God's continuing concern for the nations. At times Israel acknowledged the first evidence. Seldom did Israel accept the consequences of the second, even though the nations learned the lesson of fear (5:1).

Divine acts as judgment

God's acts in history did not always bring immediate positive results for Israel. The lesson of the wilderness stood always before them. In Egypt and in the wilderness Israel had become a disgrace. In God's purposes "the men of war coming out of Egypt were finished off who did not listen obediently to the voice of Yahweh" (5:6). God could work in history to judge Israel as well as to give them victory. Judging Israel did not mean cutting off Israel. Just as he let a generation die in the wilderness, so he raised up a new generation to accomplish his plans and possess the land (5:7). God's actions did not lead to a corner where God had no new options. God's actions led to a people who were willing to let him work with and through them to accomplish his purposes. The meaning of God's acts in history was not always clear to God's people or even to God's chosen leader. Especially was this true of God's acts of judgment.

Such acts apparently threatened God's people. After the initial defeat at Ai, Joshua had no doubt God was still a Lord of all the earth, active in history. The problem was in how the Lord was acting. Had he played a treacherous trick on Israel, planning to destroy them rather than give them the land? Joshua asked, "Alas, O Lord Yahweh, why have you so certainly caused this people to pass over the Jordan to give us into the hand of the Amorites to bring about our destruction?" (7:7). Such honest, straightforward conversation with God proved the only way to learn his plans and the meaning of his actions. Human logic concluded that Yahweh had reversed the course of all he had done. The confession of faith evoked by the gossip channels' report of Yahweh's deeds would turn to derision. Worse, it would mean defeat for God's people and thus great damage among the nations to Yahweh's reputation (7:9). Certainly, that was not God's purpose. God responded to Joshua to show the problem.

Divine acts and covenant

God's acts in history grow out of the covenant relationship. God did not act in a capricious way, one time helping Israel, the next defeating them in random fashion. God worked as Israel's covenant partner. Israel sinned. They broke the covenant.

That meant one thing. "The sons of Israel turn their backs to their enemies because they have become banned goods" (7:12).

As seen in the discussion above, Israel executed the ban as God's way of giving them the land. When Israel failed to execute the ban, Israel became banned. Israel had to deal with the sin, the breaking of covenant in their midst, before they could expect Yahweh to act in history on their behalf. This theme, though difficult to explain, is important in Joshua and through the Old Testament. Covenant obedience does not earn God's support in battle. Israel does not come before God with claims on God: You must act as we want because we have acted as the covenant laid out.

Both as obedient people and as disobedient people, Israel comes before God as a dependent people. His actions have preceded their knowledge of him. His actions have made them his servants long before they have entered his covenant. Covenant obedience is a response to previous divine action. Covenant obedience does not make demands upon God. Covenant obedience maintains the relationship in which God can continue the actions for his people which he had earlier begun and promised. Covenant disobedience severs the relationship, leading God to act in a new way. God's action is now one of action to restore the relationship rather than to maintain his saving works for his people, works which continue the fulfillment of his purposes and promises.

To continue to be the agent and recipient of God's saving acts, Israel had to find God's way of restoring the covenant relationship. God graciously pointed the way to restoration. The way of restoration may seem harsh. The sinner had made himself an enemy of God. Thus, he had to be treated as the other enemies who lived in the land. He had to become part of the banned goods and suffer the destruction all banned goods suffered (7:15). Even the one who suffered such punishment recognized its justice. Therefore, prior to punishment, he had to "set forth glory to Yahweh, the God of Israel, and give him praise" (7:19).

The act of punishment thus witnessed to God's justice and to his right to expect praise from his people. When the ban was completed, the way to covenant renewal was again open. That way led through renewed battle and victory, showing God acting again for Israel, and through Shechem and covenant renewal worship, in which Israel as a whole committed themselves anew to the covenant relationship. Thus Israel learned the nature of God's wonders, God's saving acts in their history. Historical acts begin in God's plans for his people. They embrace the people into the covenant relationship which God initiates and the people freely accept. The acts continue as they complete God's purpose, fulfill his promises to the fathers, and testify to the covenant relationship with his faithful people.

Different kinds of divine acts

God acts for his people in history in different ways. The people of Israel performed elaborate ritual acts at Jericho. The walls fell flat. The text does not explicitly say God made the walls fall, but certainly that is what the reader is expected to understand (6:20). Joshua executed intricate military strategy in the second battle of Ai, but the result was already known, for "I have given into your hand the King of The Ruin and his people and his city and his land" (8:1).

God even gave explicit military instructions (8:18). When Adoni-Zedek of Jerusalem and his southern coalition challenged Joshua, "Yahweh threw them into a panic" (10:10; compare Exod 14; Judg 4; 1 Sam 7). This set them up for Israel to destroy them. God participated in this, too, sending down well-aimed hailstones to kill the enemy and not harm Israel (10:11). Joshua asked for more. He needed daylight to complete his mission. God supplied the daylight by acting against the gods of the enemies. He made the sun and moon stand still in the sky (10:13). Thus, God acted through Joshua to show his power over the symbols of the great gods of the enemies.

One sentence summarized all this, "There has never been a day like it before or since when Yahweh listened to the voice of man, for Yahweh fought for Israel" (10:14). God could fight for his people by listening to and bringing to pass the prayer of his leader. Joshua could even promise the Israelite chiefs that "Yahweh will act accordingly against all your enemies whenever you are fighting them" (10:25). The promise came true. "All these kings and their land Joshua captured at one time because Yahweh, the God of Israel, fought for Israel" (10:42).

Fighting the enemies of his people is part of the nature of Yahweh. He may use various ways to accomplish the task. He may let the human leader gain glory as well as himself (6:27). He may use what we would call natural miracles as in the falling of the Jericho walls or 'suspending the movement' of the heavenly bodies. He may simply use good military strategy as in the defeat of Ai or the pursuit of the southern kings and the destruction of the northern kings. The means are not important. The central theme is that Yahweh carries out his plans for his people, acting for them in ways they cannot act for themselves.

Divine love and divine destruction

Such language causes problems for many people. They do not want to talk of a God who wages war. They want only to speak of a God who loves. It is somehow more satisfying to the human mind to have a God who calls for us to love and who demonstrates that love continuously.

The question must be raised: How is love demonstrated in an imperfect world filled with human evil and satanic powers? Does love not demonstrate itself in opposing such evil, in defeating evil and allowing the powers of good and love to prevail? But, the retort comes, how can defeating a whole country of people, including women and children and animals, be part of a plan of love, a plan of making God's good prevail and doing away with evil? The question allows no quick, slick, simple answer. Human logic does not have the power to justify the slaying of innocents. Human power does not have the right to take one historical example and use it as a precedence case for following the same strategy in a different human situation. That the Bible reports one instance of God using force to rid the world of evil nations does not justify people using God's name and military means to fight current battles and destroy current populations.

At most, the biblical theologian must in faith say that God's ways of dealing with evil are justified because God is just. In the fighting of the conquest, God demonstrated clearly that he is willing and able to become involved in the most difficult situations his people face. He is willing to participate in the situations filled with moral uncertainty just as much as he is willing to participate in situations where love and good obviously prevail.

God does not isolate his actions to those places and times where his goodness and love can obviously and easily reveal themselves. He also acts in cases where humanity sees only darkness and despair. He operates, however, in light of eternal plans, plans of which humans can know only in part. God's justice and goodness can be judged only on the basis of such plans and only on the basis of his eternal definitions, not on the basis of our finite viewpoints and our limited definitions.

The book of Joshua explicitly raises the moral problem a notch further: "For it had been Yahweh's idea to harden their hearts to encounter Israel in battle in order that they could put them to the ban without their having opportunity to plead for mercy. Indeed this was so that they might annihilate them just as Yahweh commanded Moses" (11:20). God caused people to oppose his people and have no opportunity to become a part of his people. Can this be justified? Has the book of Joshua presented a less than biblical view of God? Is this the Old Testament God working in ways far beneath that of the New Testament Father of our Lord Jesus Christ? Or have we missed the inspired narrative's point?

The focus is on what God has done for his people Israel.

Israelite obedience was made easier by God, who caused the inhabitants of the land to resist any temptation to plead for peace. . . . Here is a biblical lesson which has always been difficult for the people of God to learn. Deuteronomy commanded Israel to obey God, destroy the inhabitants, have no mercy, make no covenant, make no marriages (7:1–3). Such a command had a divine purpose. It removed the temptations to follow other gods. From the days of the Judges and especially from the period of Solomon onward, the great temptation was to make political alliances through covenants and political marriages between royal families (1 Kgs 11:1–8; 16:31; 20:30–43). To protect Israel against the major sin of idolatry, God commanded her not to show mercy to the enemy. To enable her to keep his commandment, God caused her enemies to fight her rather than seek mercy and peace (WBC 7:130).

God's actions in history encompassed more than simply working through Israel to bring his plans to pass. He worked in the hearts of even the enemies to accomplish his purposes. In this way, too, he showed that he was, indeed, Lord of all the earth. No people could withstand him. He could work with them in any way he chose. He was sovereign even over the mental capacities of the enemies. Because of this, Israel could testify, "Not a single man stood before them from all their enemies; rather all their enemies, Yahweh gave into their hand. Not a single word fell from every good word which Yahweh spoke to the house of Israel. Everything came to pass" (23:44–45).

Divine acts and future generations

God's acts in history are not limited to one particular era. He worked through Joshua to give Israel the land. Joshua became old and advanced in years, ready to retire from the conquest task. God led him to retire, but only after Yahweh promised to keep up the fight: "all the inhabitants of the hill country from Lebanon unto Misraphoth Mayim, all the Sidonians, I will dispossess them before the sons of Israel, only cause it to fall to Israel for an inheritance just as I commanded you" (13:6).

The era of Joshua would pass. The fighting of Yahweh for his people would continue. God's purposes would come to pass despite the passing of mighty leaders. Neither Moses nor Joshua was necessary for God to act in history. God could and would act how and when he chose. The remainder of the Bible and of human history testifies to this. God has acted, acts, and will continue to act for his people to bring his purpose to completions. This is biblical testimony.

Modern historians and philosophers of language have a problem with such statements. They want history to be the realm of human actions and thus expect the historian to explain events through the rules of cause and effect, rules that presumably can be repeated in similar circumstances. They do not necessarily want to eliminate faith and God from human discussion. They simply want to bracket God out of the discussion when they are doing scientific history. Thus, they may not want to give the title *history writing* to a book such as Joshua. It becomes simply a source book for the modern historian to use in reconstructing history, but cannot be graced with the title a work of history. Such treatment of the book of Joshua and its events can be defended by human logic and with specific definitions of history. Such logic and rules of definition ignore the biblical perspective on history and the biblical view of God.

The Bible refuses to isolate God in his heavenly palace, aloof from the actions of human history. Likewise, the Bible refuses to grant humans the power to explain all events on earth through the rules of cause and effect. The Bible portrays history in the language of faith, not in the language of the "scientific historian." The language of faith sees more at work than does the language of the "scientific historian." The language of faith sees human history as a cooperative effort between God and his people to establish divine purposes. It sees God working to empower his people to accomplish his purposes. It sees God as the primary cause of human history. This is not to say God is the only cause and that human actions are always divinely caused. The Bible goes to great lengths to describe human pride and rebellion in its exercise of freedom to oppose divine plans and actions. The Bible thus describes human history as a battleground in which forces of evil combat God for the minds, the wills, the hearts of people. Both the forces of evil and God work through human agency to accomplish their purposes.

History is not simply a battle between God and Satan. History encompasses all human actions. Human actions are not, however, simple actions resulting from totally free human decisions. Human actions are actions resulting from people with commitments. Some human commitments are to other human beings in love, trust, and joint action. Some human commitments are to powers of evil in outright rebellion against what the person knows to be right and good. Some human commitments are to God and his purposes. The complex interactions of these human commitments—which may all lie in the depths of a single individual—eventually give the impetus to human history. Explanation of human commitment, human will, human decision-making requires more than mere descriptions of cause and effect. Such explanation also invokes those forces that work to influence such commitments. The Bible and Christian faith hold to God as a major Actor in such explanations. The Bible and Christian faith go further. They hold that God is not content simply to work through human beings. At times God chooses to work within the events of history. No video camera can record such actions. No physical eye can describe the hows and wherefores of such actions. On the other side, some events are beyond human imagination. No human causes suffice to explain the events.

The major such event is the resurrection of Jesus of Nazareth. Once the reality of that event is granted, the possibility of God's actions in human history cannot be denied. The question then becomes not, does God work in history? but, in what ways does he work and in what events has he worked? The biblical record testifies to many events in which God works. The language of faith then extends that testimony to say that the possibility, yea, the probability, exists that God continues to work in human history.

God who makes demands

God speaks. God acts in history. God makes demands. The covenant relationship is not a one-sided relationship with no expectations on Israel. Rather, the relationship makes impossible demands.

"You are not able to serve Yahweh, because a holy God is he, a jealous deity is he, one who will not forgive your sins and transgressions. If you should forsake Yahweh and serve strange, foreign gods, he will turn and do evil to you. He will finish you off after having been so good to you." (24:19–20)

This part of God's nature provides the tension of the biblical narrative. An all-giving, always forgiving god would make no demands on the people. The people would stand under no threat. The conclusion of the story would be assured from the first. Threat, punishment, loss of power, exile would all be impossible. The story would feature one victory after another by a self-indulgent people. God is not like that, so the story is not like that. Israel's story is one of trying to meet God's demands, a story with tremendous successes and horrendous failures. The book of Joshua has its share of both.

God makes leadership demands. To be leader of God's people is not a position of honor to be enjoyed and rewarded. The leader of God's people must listen to the demands of God.

Leadership in Israel is leadership following God's orders, not unfettered leadership accomplishing personal desires. At every turn Joshua turned to Yahweh for direction prior to issuing orders to the people. Yahweh's orders did not always follow the dictates of human reason. Cross a flooded river. March openly around a walled city for seven days. Circumcise adult males. Search out and destroy a family of your own people. Make a strong, wily enemy people servants in your own worship place with daily contact with government officials. Stop the successful conquest in the final phases just because the leader is getting old. Take important cities away from tribes to give them to priests. Such demands would not fill the pages of military strategy published by most military academies. They did fill God's strategy demands on Joshua.

The demands of leadership continued away from the field of action. God called on Joshua to study the Torah of Moses continually. The leader had to subject himself to religious tradition, to the teachings of his predecessor. The leader was not called on to initiate brilliant strategy of his own and to reformulate the expectations of the people in his own image. Rather, the leader had to carry on the methods and demands of the previous generation of leadership. New leaders expect the right to create new leadership styles and new directions for the people. Leaders want to place their own imprint on the life and history of the people. Joshua was called to imitate and continue more of the same much more than to set personal, individual marks on the nation's history.

Leadership demands called for courage and strength. Joshua had to become the first role model for Israel's leadership in the shadow of Moses and his Torah. As such, he had to trace a path unlike that the people might expect. They would look for leaders like those in Egypt or in Canaan. They would look for strong personal initiative. They would expect a leader who exhibited his power for all to see to impress his own people and the enemy. Yahweh demanded that Joshua retreat to the study with the

Torah of Moses. Did it take more courage to follow the Near Eastern leadership role model or the Mosaic model?

Joshua also had to lead a people not fully committed to the Mosaic Law, as the example of Achan showed quite early. Did Joshua have the courage to enforce the Law of Moses in the face of popular opposition? Was Joshua willing to stake his leadership on God's demands and directions, or would he compromise those demands to satisfy the desires of the people? Leadership demands placed Joshua against Near Eastern models, against personal desires of the people, and against political and military situations with seemingly little chance of success. Could he face these and meet God's basic command: "Have I not commanded you, 'Have conviction and courage. Do not tremble or get all shook up, for with you is Yahweh your God everywhere you go'?" (1:9). Was God's promise of his presence sufficient reason to follow his leadership demands in face of other leadership styles and demands?

That was the basic question Joshua faced. The book of Joshua illustrates Joshua's faithfulness in following God's demands. He listened to divine orders, relayed these to his leadership staff or to the people, and carried them out just as they were given. He thus became a role model for all future leaders of God's people. This became clear in his very first confrontation with the people. He faced the group most likely to give him trouble, the people from East of Jordan who already had their assigned territories and had no obvious reason to cross the Jordan and continue the battle. Joshua showed them he knew the Torah of Moses. He also showed them he had a plan for the future, a plan which made further demands on their time and commitment to the people Israel. They swore allegiance to him, recognizing that he continued the leadership style of Moses: "According to all the way in which we have obeyed Moses, so we will obey you. . . . Every man who rebels against your order and does not obey your words to the last detail which you command us shall be put to death" (1:17–18).

The people East of Jordan recognized one need in Joshua's life, the same need Yahweh had pointed out—conviction and courage (1:18; compare vv. 6, 7, 9). A courageous leader who stuck to his convictions could meet Yahweh's leadership demands. Such a leader could expect the followship of God's people. Such a leader had to meet one other implied demand of God: He had to recognize that he was not the fully-empowered, independent leader. Yahweh had a heavenly army much more powerful than any earthly army. That army had a "prince of the host of Yahweh" (5:14). Joshua had to obey commands from on high and recognize leadership higher than his own before he could effectively issue commands to God's people. Joshua led the earthly hierarchy, but he stood in a chain of command. He had to obey a higher general's orders.

Ritual demands

Yahweh also had ritual demands. The reader of Joshua comes away with memories of battles and conquest. The student of the structure of the book of Joshua realizes that religious ritual surrounds, and to a large extent dominates, the stories of battle and conquest. Priests lead the way through the Jordan and around Jericho.

Circumcision, Passover, and acknowledgement of holy ground prepare the way to Jericho. Prayer and religious ritual determine the fate of Achan and enable Israel to rebound from defeat to capture Ai. Rededication to the Torah of Moses and covenant of God interrupt the conquest narrative almost before it has begun. The priest and the lot play an important role in the distribution of territories to the tribes. The process is interrupted as the tribes regather at Shiloh around the tent of meeting.

The death of the high priest plays a crucial role in the law of the cities of refuge. The last distribution of territory is to the levitic priests. The final story of the book is a dispute over the place

of worship, settled by the priest. The final actions are a covenant sermon and covenant renewal ceremony. The demands
of worship thus dominate the structure of Joshua and probably
should dominate the themes we study from the book to a greater
extent than they usually do.

1. *Study of Torah.* Yahweh's first ritual demand is the study
of Torah. This is for the leader, Joshua, but it is also for the
people. Covenant renewal is time for lessons in Torah (chs 8;
24). The people must know God's history with his people and God's
expectations of his people. Because the people know both
God's actions and God's demands, they are ready to commit
themselves to obey God's covenant demands:

> "Far be it from us, the forsaking of Yahweh to serve other
> gods, for Yahweh is our God. He is the one who brought
> us up and our fathers from the land of Egypt, from the
> house of service, and who did before our eyes these great
> signs. He protected us in all the way in which we went and
> among all the peoples through whose midst we passed.
> Yahweh drove out all the peoples, indeed the Amorite
> living in the land, from before us. Yes, we also will serve
> Yahweh, because He is our God." (24:16–18)

The study of Torah leads the people to know God, his acts,
and his demands. Such knowledge results in a pledge to serve
God and meet his requirements. In ritual God's people learn
and give themselves to the God who demands.

2. *Leadership of priests.* Yahweh's second ritual demand is the
leadership of priests. Joshua was the leader, but he had constantly to recognize the important role of religious leaders. The
priests led through the Jordan. The priests led around Jericho.
The priests participated in the distribution of land. The priests
mediated the dispute over the worship place of the East Jordan
tribes. The priests lived among each of the tribes. Political and
military leadership was not enough. God had reserved certain

places for the priests. Leaders such as Joshua had to recognize the priests' role and encourage them in performing that role. An important part of that role was to keep before the people the ark of the covenant, symbolizing the presence of God. Priests, not Joshua, had charge of the worship place and the symbol of God being with his people. In his demands, God had divided leadership responsibility. Leaders had to accept God's way of dividing leadership rather than seeking to gain more power at the expense of someone else. Joshua provided a role model in letting the priests exercise their prescribed functions while limiting himself to those areas in which God gave him leadership authority.

3. *Worship requirements.* The third ritual demand centered on worship requirements. God expected male members of the community to undergo circumcision as a sign of the covenant people of Abraham and as a symbol of a new generation committed to the demands of Yahweh and cleansed by Yahweh. Circumcision was done in the traditional way God expected—with flint knives rather than the newly-invented metal ones. He expected them to keep Passover, remembering God's acts in Egypt and committing themselves to till the land and depend upon its fruits for their food. God expected them to worship where he chose. Thus they went to Shechem to renew the covenant. Likewise the East Jordan tribes' altar was a witness but not an altar of worship. Also, the tent of meeting was set up, and the second portion of the distribution of the land occurred at Shiloh. Worship was not a human plan displaying human capabilities to God. Worship was a human response to God's great acts, a response made following the way God had demanded.

4. *Covenant demands.* The final ritual demand centered on covenant. This was an extension of the worship demand and has been discussed above under loyalty. God expected his people to gather at Shechem and renew the covenant, learning anew God's demands and committing themselves to those demands. Here Israel gained identity as the people of the God who had

acted in their history and thus had the right to make covenant demands, which they willingly chose to follow.

Ethical demands

God's demands could be summarized as ethical demands. The center of Torah demands were ethical. The book of Joshua summarizes these in one sentence:

"Only, be exceedingly careful to obey the commandments and the Torah, which Moses, the servant of Yahweh, commanded you, to love Yahweh, your God, and to walk in all his ways and to obey his commandments and to cleave to him and to serve him with all your heart and with all your being." (22:5)

God's demands are not based on a tyrant/helpless vassal relationship. They are based on a relationship between a God of love whose people love him in return. This love of God shows itself in all he has done for his people, calling the patriarchs, freeing the slaves in Egypt, making the covenant, guiding the people through the wilderness, and giving them the land.

His love is also shown in his anger and jealousy. God's anger burns against his covenant people when they break the covenant (7:1). God's anger guards the trust relationship. Israel broke the trust relationship they had with God. They refused to do what they had committed themselves to do. They stole part of the banned goods they had devoted to Yahweh. Anger is the response to a breach of that trust. Anger is the response that shows God takes the relationship seriously and expects the agreed-upon demands of the relationship to be fulfilled. Not to react in anger would mean that God had not intended for Israel to take the relationship seriously and that God did not take the relationship seriously. Lack of anger would mean shallow commitment. Absence of anger would mean the relationship could be an off-again, on-again arrangement at either party's whim. The covenant was not simply a business deal with both parties signing a contract for a specified time or until a better deal came along. The covenant was an emotional commitment of the very heart and being of God and of Israel.

Such emotional commitments bring emotional responses when they are broken. Israel learned the hard way that God took the covenant commitment seriously and responded in burning anger when Israel refused to take it seriously. Anger was not an eternal emotion of God. God showed Israel how to respond to his anger. He provided ritual action, indeed radical ritual action, Israel could take (ch 7). When Israel did take the covenant relationship seriously enough to fall on her knees before God and seek to renew the relationship, then God led them back in the way. When Israel followed God's way back, then "Yahweh repented of his burning rage" (7:26).

God's jealousy is another part of his emotional attachment to the covenant people. Jealousy in our terms is the reaction of a lover against the person who steals the heart of the beloved. The Canaanites attributed such emotions to their gods. Rival gods entered into lovers' quarrels. For Yahweh, jealousy took another turn: It was both jealous and zealous. In his zeal to protect and maintain his love relationship with Israel, God placed demands upon his beloved people. He expected them to be holy, morally pure and perfect, just as he was. He expected them to be faithful, committed only to him as he was committed only to them.

> He loves them so much that he wants their undivided love in return. He will not share them with any other god. God turns his jealous indignation against the unfaithful worshiper, not against the rival lover. He punishes the people who try to serve him along with some other god. God's jealousy cannot tolerate this. He has given undivided love and wants the same from them (cf. Exod 20:5; 34:14–16). (WBC 7:275)

Uniquely, the jealousy of God means God's people cannot serve him: "You are not able to serve Yahweh, because a holy God is he, a jealous deity is he, one who will not forgive your sins and transgressions" (24:19).

The nature of God himself prevents Israel from serving him. His holy purity and jealous love both tie him in total devotion to his people and tie them off from fulfilling his demands. This has drastic consequences. God will not forgive Israel's sins (cf. Exod 23:21). His expectations of them are too high. His love for them is too great. He cannot easily ignore their wrongdoings, their casual flirtations with other gods. The gods of the neighbors would simply wait for the worshiper to come back. Yahweh goes out to discipline the errant lover until she returns. (WBC 7:275)

Still, Israel does not think these demands are too high. In face of the warning of God's holy jealousy, Israel insists, "No, but it is Yahweh we will serve!" The holy jealousy of God is not a repulsive attribute which terrifies His people. It is part of the attraction of God. Only a God who expects so much and loves so exclusively can fulfill our expectations. We do not want to worship one who loves and leaves as we do. We commit ourselves to the One whose expectations are so high we can never fulfill them, but whose nature is so perfect that He can expect and demand no less because He expects and performs those demands for Himself.

God is faithful

God expects his leader and his people to know and follow Torah. Central to Torah are the promises God made to the fathers. As seen above, the gift of land is basic to these promises. God has not truly created a people until he has given them land of their own to till and rule independently of any other peoples or nation. The book of Joshua centers on this aspect of God. God's speech, opening the book, promises,

> "Every place where the sole of your foot steps, to you I have given it, precisely as I told Moses. . . . it is you who will cause this people to inherit the land which I made an oath with their fathers to give to them." (1:3, 6)

God faithfully remembers the promises of Torah just as he expects the people to remember the demands of Torah. God promised to fulfill that oath to the fathers, but only to a faithful generation (5:6). The generation of Joshua was the faithful generation. "Joshua took all the land, according to all which Yahweh spoke to Moses" (11:22). The climax of the conquest narrative reaffirms this: "Yahweh gave to Israel all the land which he had sworn to give to their fathers, and they possessed it and lived in it. Yahweh gave them rest all around, according to everything which he had sworn to their fathers. . . . Not a single word fell from every good word which Yahweh spoke to the house of Israel. Everything came to pass" (21:43–45).

If we had to isolate from the conquest narratives of the book of Joshua the one theme the writer wished to impress upon the readers, it was this: Yahweh has done his part. He is faithful. You can see what he has done in the past. You know you can trust him for the future.

The corollary to this theme is similar: If you are in trouble, you cannot blame Yahweh. Past history shows his nature. He is faithful to keep his promises.

The book of Joshua goes even one step further. If you are in trouble, you had better look at Yahweh's demands and your faithfulness. Why? Because Yahweh is not only faithful to his promises. He is also faithful to his warnings:

> "You all know with all your hearts and with all your being that not one word has fallen from all the good words which

Yahweh, your God, spoke concerning you. They all have come to pass for you. Not one word has fallen from among them. And it will be the case that just as every good word which Yahweh, your God, spoke to you has come upon you just so Yahweh will bring upon you every evil word until he has destroyed you from upon this good land which Yahweh, your God, has given to you. When you transgress the covenant of Yahweh, your God, that he commanded you, and you go off and serve other gods and bow down in worship to them, then the anger of Yahweh will burn against you and you will quickly wander away lost from upon this good land which he has given to you." (21:14–16)

God is faithful to his promises and to his threats. The lesson is clear. His people must be faithful, too.

God is present

God's faithfulness shows itself in his presence.[13] The theme of presence is the repeated sign in chapter 1. God promised Joshua victory over all his enemies. The only evidence Joshua had that victory would actually come was the promise of God's presence (1:5). That presence was not a new theme. Joshua had seen evidence of God's presence previously, for it was the power of presence with Moses. Leadership in Israel had one necessary quality. The leader had to have God's presence, the same presence that had been with Moses. The presence was an unlimited presence. Joshua did not have to go to the place of worship. He did not have to be sure the priests were with him. He did not have to ensure he had taken the ark of covenant. Sanctuary, priests, ark . . . all could symbolize God's presence, but none was necessary. God was present "everywhere you go" (1:9).

Thus, Joshua could have conviction and courage. He had no reason to tremble or to lose heart. He never had to rely on his own power and ability. He always had God's power and ability to call upon. God called his leader to service, but that was never solitary service. It was always service in the eternal presence of God.

Israel expected God to be present with their leader. The East Jordan tribes answered Joshua's call to cross the Jordan with a united Israel with one demand: "According to all the way in which we have obeyed Moses, so we will obey you. Only let Yahweh your God be with you just as he was with Moses" (1:17). Joshua had to lead just as Moses had led. Joshua could not presume to lead in his own strength. He had to lead in the strength of the One who had been with Moses. Joshua could meet that condition. Yahweh had made that promise in calling Joshua to service.

The understanding that God was present with his people had a long history in Israel. It rooted in the life of the patriarchs. God promised to be with them on their long, fearful journeys through unknown territories (Gen 28:15; 31:3; Exod 3:12). The theme was part of Israel's understanding of holy war, war in which God directed his people to carry out certain instructions such as the ban and in which he promised to lead them with his presence. This is the meaning in the opening chapter of Joshua in its more limited sense (compare Num 14:43; Judg 6:11–16; 1 Sam 17:37; 2 Sam 7:9). Thus, the theme of divine presence appears in the laws of Deuteronomy only in the laws for battle (Deut 20:1–4). The narrative of Deuteronomy speaks of God's presence in the wilderness wanderings (2:7) and in Joshua's preparation for conquest (31:6, 8, 23). The theme of divine presence

> expresses one of the basic roots of Israelite faith, the belief that Yahweh is the God of Israel who accompanies, leads, protects, fights, and goes with the men he has chosen for his work. (WBC 7:12)

Divine presence was not simply an invisible, unprovable promise. Divine presence brought specific accomplishments. For

Joshua, this meant victory in battle—victory the people could see.

God used the victory to do two things in the midst of the people of Israel. He made Joshua great, and he gave evidence that his presence was with Joshua just as it had been with Moses (3:7). This at least implies a definition of human greatness for Israel. Israel could recognize human greatness through achievements of the human leader, but Israel knew that those achievements did not come through the leader's own ability and skill. Those achievements pointed beyond the leader. They pointed to God and his presence. Human greatness was a direct result of divine presence. This meant that human greatness brought recognition for the individual, but its basic result was to bring praise to God.

The great human was simply an agent allowing God to work out his purposes and achieve his plans through his presence. To recognize that presence, Israel turned to its original great hero—Moses. Israel knew the story of Moses and what he had accomplished. Israel knew that those accomplishments came through the presence of Yahweh. Anytime another Israelite leader accomplished acts similar to Moses' feats, Israel knew God was present with that leader. The leader did not take time to revel in his own greatness. Instead, he or she gave credit to God's presence and turned to the next task in God's commands.

In Joshua's case the evidence for divine presence was simple. Yahweh would drive out the inhabitants of the promised land. Then Israel would know beyond any doubt that the living God, Yahweh, the God of Israel, was present among his people (3:10). The battle of Jericho presented the first clear piece of evidence. There "Yahweh was with Joshua, and his reputation was in all the land" (6:27). This implies that Joshua's feat at Jericho did more than show Israel that Yahweh was present with him and among them. It witnessed to everyone in the land of Canaan that Yahweh was with Joshua, building Joshua's reputation. One may even take the statement a step further. As seen above, in

Hebrew "land" and "earth" are the same word. The writer of the book of Joshua may have intended for the readers to see the full implication of what Yahweh was doing through Joshua. Yahweh was making Joshua's name great and thus proving his divine presence throughout the entire earth.

Presence of God was not an unconditional, eternal guarantee. God's presence came to a faithful covenant people. When Israel broke the covenant, they heard a different kind of word from Yahweh: "Never again will I be with you if you do not banish the banned goods from your midst" (7:12). Instead of enforcing God's ban on the goods captured in Jericho, Israel in the person of Achan had taken some of the banned goods for themselves. This transformed Israel into "banned goods." A people under the ban could not expect the presence of God with them. The holy God could not be present with a sinful people. The presence of the holy God with banned goods led to the destruction of the banned goods. Apparently, the whole plan of the book of Joshua could not be accomplished. Israel had refused to be the faithful generation which could experience God's presence.

> The key promise to Joshua in the book is the presence of God. Divine presence is the prayer of the people for Joshua, the basis of Joshua's exaltation, and the hope of possessing the land. Passing over the covenant has let all this pass away. All is not totally hopeless. There is a big 'if.' Obedient people will destroy the banned goods in their midst and again experience divine presence. Israel must choose between the presence of God and the presence of banned goods. (WBC 7:85)

To experience the divine presence, Israel had to be the people of the covenant. Otherwise they were choosing to be the people of the covenant curses. To be God's people is to experience God's presence. Not to experience God's presence is to be banned goods, apart from God, under the covenant curse, and in danger of destruction which was the eventual fate of banned goods.

Joshua did not have a monopoly on divine presence. God promised his presence to leaders carrying out his purpose. Caleb called on the divine presence as the guarantee of his success in driving the mighty Anakim out of Hebron and other cities (14:12). Phinehas, the priest, could testify to God's presence among all the people as a result of solving the threatened civil war between East and West Jordan tribes. When it became evident that no wrong had been committed and the tribes were still united in purpose, the priest declared, "Today we know that Yahweh is in our midst, because you have not disobeyed Yahweh in this disobedience. In that way, you have delivered the sons of Israel from the hand of Yahweh" (22:31).

Disobedient Israel would have to face the threat of divine punishment. Obedient Israel could live in the blessing and protection of the presence of Yahweh. That presence not only led God's people as they traveled in unknown places and guaranteed victory as God led his people into battle. That presence also witnessed to the unity and obedience of his people. That presence guided the people to solve problems which threatened the very life of the nation.

Amidst the arguments of men, the promised presence of God reveals itself and brings peace. (WBC 7:249)

For the book of Joshua, God is the One who speaks, who demands, who acts in history, who is faithful, and, above all, who is present with his people. It is this God who makes covenant with his people and guides them to victory over the people of the promised land and who leads them to distribute the land fairly among the tribes. It is this God who calls them to service even knowing they cannot meet his zealous, jealous demands, nor escape his anger, and must face the threat of loss of land and exile. Still, this God is so great and perfect that Israel can only commit themselves to serve him, knowing the impossibility of the task. God accepts such a people as his covenant people and seeks to lead them further along the path to accomplish his purposes.

EPILOG
THE PEOPLE OF GOD

The Old Testament as a whole, and the book of Joshua in particular, have a wide variety of themes. In the pages above, we have been able to touch on only a few of those topics. Study of the individual themes, however, does not tell the whole story. One must look further than the individual parts. One must ask the purpose, the intention of the whole. Having looked at leadership, land, law, loyalty, and Lord, we still do not have the larger picture. What is the total theme, the overarching goal of the book of Joshua?

The present writer thinks the goal of the book, and quite probably of the Old Testament as a whole, is to give identity to the people of God.[14] The Bible is written by members of the people of God to a larger group. This larger group claims to be people of God. In the eyes of the inspired writer, however, they do not all give evidence of the marks of God's people. The inspired book of Joshua in its entirety provides a standard with which people who claim to be a part of God's covenant people can examine themselves and see if they really meet God's test. That test involves a series of questions.

1. Have you committed yourself to the covenant God has made with his people? For Israel this was a public commitment as part of the people of God. It involved the ceremonies apparent in 8:30–35 and in chapter 24. It meant having listened to the entire Torah of God read publicly. It meant having rehearsed God's history with his people. It meant knowing the serious nature of being the people of the God who expressed himself not only in presence and love but also in anger and jealousy. It meant saying publicly with God's people, "Yahweh, our God, we will serve. His voice we will obey" (24:24).

2. Are you willing to accept the consequences of that commitment? Commitment to Yahweh sets you off from all your neighbors. They had freedom to worship all the gods they could find—to participate in the exciting, alluring worship rituals connected with the fertility gods. They had freedom to go to another god for help when the god they were calling on did not seem to be able to give help at the present moment in the present kind of need. In freedom they could call on the ancient traditions of the land, which seemed to have worked well enough for many generations. They could worship at the many ancient worship places which had been used in the land for centuries. They did not have to limit themselves to the one place Yahweh chose for them. They were free to use their creative talents to form images of their gods and ensure the presence of those gods among them.

To commit oneself to the covenant of Yahweh was to give up all these freedoms and to worship where Yahweh said to worship without any image to ensure that Yahweh was even present. It was to agree to worship him and him alone, knowing the threats Yahweh had made against those unfaithful to him:

> "You are not able to serve Yahweh, because a holy God is he, a jealous deity is he, one who will not forgive your sins and transgressions. If you should forsake Yahweh and serve strange, foreign gods, he will turn and do evil to you.

He will finish you off after having been so good to you all." (24:19–20)

3. *Do you know why you serve Yahweh?* Yahweh is different from all other gods. He is not limited to one area of life. He is not just the god of the sun or the god of fertility or the god of the household or the god of war.

Yahweh is the God who proved his power when he had no people, when the fathers had other gods whom they "served beyond the rivers and in Egypt" (24:14).

Yahweh is the God who could begin to build his kingdom with one person: "I took your father Abraham from beyond the river and caused him to go through all the land of Canaan" (24:3).

Yahweh is the only God of fertility. "I multiplied his seed" (24:3), fulfilling his promise to Abraham and the fathers and producing the nation of Israel.

Yahweh is the God of the wanderer, leading Abraham from Mesopotamia to Canaan and Israel from Egypt through the wilderness (compare 24:3, 7).

Yahweh is the God over the nations. Israel's enemies had two major homes—Mesopotamia and Egypt. Yahweh took Abraham from Mesopotamia and Israel from Egypt. In Canaan, Israel faced smaller enemies all around. "I gave to Esau [the Edomites] Mount Seir" (24:4). "I brought you all to the land of the Amorites, the ones who dwell beyond the Jordan. They fought you, and I gave them into your hand. You possessed their land" (24:7–8).

Yahweh is the God over all prophets. "Balak, . . . king of Moab, rose and fought against Israel. He sent and called Balaam, the son of Beor, to curse you. But I did not consent to listen to Balaam, and he actually blessed you. I delivered you from his hand" (24:9–10).

Yahweh is the God of war. "I struck Egypt. . . . Your eyes saw what I did in Egypt. . . . The lords of Jericho—the Amorites, the Perizzites, the Canaanites, the Hittites, the Girgashites, and the Hivites, and the Jebusites—fought against you. I gave them into your hand. . . . But it was not by your sword nor by your bow. I gave to you a land in which you did not exert yourself and cities which you did not build, and you lived in them" (24:5, 7, 11–13).

Yahweh is the God of agriculture. "(I also gave) vineyards and olive orchards, which though you did not plant, you are eating" (24:13).

Yahweh is the God who controlled the land and gave it to whom he pleased. He gave it to show his faithfulness to his word: "Yahweh gave to Israel all the land which he had sworn to give to their fathers, and they possessed it and lived in it" (21:43).

Yahweh, the Lord of all the earth and sovereign in war, is above all the God who shapes rest and peace for his people. "Yahweh gave them rest all around, according to everything which he had sworn to their fathers" (21:44).

You serve Yahweh because he is different from all other gods. His difference attracts you. His difference proves his claim to be the only God who can exert influence over your lives. His difference justifies his demand for exclusive allegiance. His difference makes you willing to choose in freedom to serve him and put aside all other gods. You serve Yahweh because of who he is and what you choose.

4. *Do you know God's Torah demands on Israel?* Have you paid attention to the covenant ceremonies? Have you realized that the reading of Torah is more than a public ritual done for pomp and circumstance? Have you seen Torah directed to you personally, calling you to embrace its demands as the lifestyle you choose, the lifestyle God has set out as the best for you? Do you see Torah as God's gracious gift to you setting out the boundary lines of life with God and giving you freedom to shape your life within those boundary lines?

Are you willing to share Torah with all those with whom God shares it—"including women and children, and the aliens active among you" (8:35)? Will you witness against yourself that you have submitted your life to Torah no matter what the consequence?

5. *Do you understand the one word that summarizes Torah?* Are you ready to make love the central characteristic of your life? "Only be exceedingly careful to obey the commandments and the Torah which Moses, the servant of Yahweh, commanded you, to love Yahweh, your God" (22:5). "You must guard yourselves carefully to love Yahweh, your God" (23:11).

Being people of God does not mean drearily keeping a series of laws in order to be good or to escape punishment. Being people of God does not mean keeping a Torah scorecard to show how good you are and stroke your pride. Nor does it mean cowering in fear, looking behind every rock, knowing that behind the next turn God will have someone waiting to jump out and get you because he found the one place you stepped across the Torah boundary.

Being people of God is being in love with the most wonderful Person you ever met. It means joyfully searching for ways to please the Beloved because of the wonder of the love that dominates your life. It is celebrating a lifelong love affair with the living God, the Lord of all the earth. Such a love affair calls for courage, for faith, and for conviction as you live in God's rest.

That is the book of Joshua, a summary of the people of God committed to the covenant, accepting the consequences of that commitment, knowing why they serve God, knowing the demands of Torah, understanding love as the center of Torah. Joshua shows how God defined and demonstrated leadership, gave land and law, demanded loyalty, and acted as Lord. Joshua holds up what once was and invites people to believe it can happen again.

NOTES

1. For a discussion of laments, see A. A. Anderson, *Psalms*, New Century Bible Commentary (London: Marshall, Morgan and Scott, 1972), I, 36–39; Claus Westermann, *Praise and Lament in the Psalms* (Atlanta: John Knox, 1981); Leslie C. Allen, *Psalms*, Word Biblical Themes (Waco, Tex.: Word, 1987), 59–74; Trent C. Butler, "Piety in the Psalms," *Review and Expositor* 81 (Summer, 1984), 385–94.

2. This is worked out more fully in Trent C. Butler, "The Form of the Book of Joshua and Its Significance for Old Testament Research," an unpublished paper delivered at the annual meeting of the Society of Biblical Literature, Anaheim, Calif., Nov., 1985.

3. See Deuteronomy commentaries for further development of these themes: John D. W. Watts, "Deuteronomy," *The Broadman Bible Commentary* (Nashville: Broadman Press, 1970), I, 175–296; Gerhard von Rad, *Deuteronomy*, The Old Testament Library (Philadelphia: The Westminster Press, 1970); P. C. Craigie, *The Book of Deuteronomy* (Grand Rapids: Wm. B. Eerdmans, 1976); A. D. H. Mayes, *Deuteronomy*, The New Century Bible Commentary (London: Marshall, Morgan, and Scott, 1979).

4. See Edward R. Dalglish, "Judges" *The Broadman Bible Commentary* (Nashville: Broadman Press, 1970), II, 377–463; J. Alberto Soggin, *Judges*, The Old Testament Library (Philadelphia, The Westminster Press, 1981); Trent C. Butler, "The Royal Theme in the Book of Judges," an unpublished paper delivered at the annual meeting of the Society of Biblical Literature, Anaheim, California, November, 1989.

5. See Ben F. Philbeck, Jr., "1 and 2 Samuel," *The Broadman Bible Commentary* (Nashville: Broadman Press, 1970), III, 1–145; Ralph W. Klein, *1 Samuel*, Word Biblical Commentary 10 (Waco, Tex.: Word, 1983).

6. See A. A. Anderson, *2 Samuel*, Word Biblical Commentary 11 (Dallas, Tex.: Word, 1989); Gerhard von Rad, *Old Testament Theology* (London: Oliver & Boyd Ltd., 1962), I, 306–26.

7. See M. Pierce Matheney, Jr., and Roy L. Honeycutt, Jr., "1 Kings" and "2 Kings," *The Broadman Bible Commentary* (Nashville: Broadman Press, 1970), 246–396; Simon J. DeVries, *1 Kings*, Word Biblical Commentary 12 (Waco, Tex.: Word, 1985); T. R. Hobbs, *2 Kings*, Word Biblical Commentary 13 (Waco, Tex.: Word, 1985).

8. For further discussion of Joshua's "office," see Word Biblical Commentary 7, 9–10.

9. On holy war theology, see Gwilym H. Jones, "The Concept of Holy War," *The World of Ancient Israel*, ed. R. E. Clements (New York: Cambridge University Press, 1989), 299–321; Elmer A. Martens, *God's Design* (Grand Rapids: Baker, 1981), 44–46, 60–63, 204–6; John H. Yoder, "'To Your Tents, O Israel': The Legacy of Israel's Experience with Holy War," *Studies in Religion* 18 (1989), 345–62.

10. For a theological discussion of law, see Brevard S. Childs, *Old Testament Theology in a Canonical Context* (Philadelphia: Fortress Press, 1985), 50–62; R. E. Clements, *Old Testament Theology* (London: Marshall, Morgan and Scott, 1978), 104–30.

11. For a discussion of covenant, see Trent C. Butler, "Covenant," *Holman Bible Dictionary* (Nashville: Holman, 1991), 308–12; R. Davidson, "Covenant Ideology in Ancient Israel," *The World of Ancient Israel*, ed. R. E. Clements (New York: Cambridge University Press, 1989), 323–48.

12. For an overview of the biblical understanding of history, see Trent C. Butler, notes and "Summary of the Doctrine of History," *Disciple's Study Bible* (Nashville: Holman, 1988), 1680–81, 1855–57.

13. Samuel Terrien, *The Elusive Presence* (San Francisco: Harper and Row, 1978), has used divine "presence" as the central theme for biblical theology.

14. For a brief overview of "people of God," see R. E. Clements, *Old Testament Theology*, 79–103.

INDEX OF SCRIPTURES

COLOSSIANS

7:6–15	79	10:13	57, 89	14:1–5	8
7:6–9	7	10:14	90	14:1	10, 27–28
7:7	37, 87	10:15–43	8	14:1–2	43
7:9	37, 87	10:19	37	14:2	61
7:10–26	7	10:25	90	14:3–4	38
7:10–15	77	10:27	30	14:5	58
7:10–13	60	10:28	47	14:6–15	8, 31
7:11–12	47	10:35	47	14:6–14	77
7:11	37, 70	10:37	47	14:6	61
7:12	88, 108	10:39	47	14:7–8	68
7:15	47, 70, 88	10:40	47, 58	14:7	25
7:19	88	10:42	90	14:9	43
7:24	29	11:1–4	8	14:12	42, 109
7:26	102	11:1	80	14:13	10, 38, 61
8:1–29	7, 99	11:5–15	8	14:14	68
8:1–2	77	11:6	37, 58, 77	14:15	49
8:1	9, 58, 60, 89	11:8	37	15:1–17:18	8
8:7	37, 41	11:9	58	15:1	61
8:18	37, 58–89	11:12	25, 47, 58	15:13	10, 61
8:26	47	11:15	25, 59	15:14	42
8:27	58	11:16–12:24	13	15:63	31, 41
8:28	30	11:16–23	8	16:1	61
8:29	30	11:20	47, 91	16:10	31, 41
8:30–35	7, 16, 19,	11:21	47	17:1	61
	31, 54, 70, 112	11:22	104	17:3–6	43
8:30	9	11:23	17–18, 41,	17:4–6	43
8:31	25		49, 59	17:4	10, 28
8:33–35	54	12:1–24	8, 12	17:12–13	41
8:33	25, 27, 55	12:1–6	66	17:14–18	10
8:35	54, 114	12:1	41	17:14	39, 43, 61
9:1–3	10	12:6	25, 41	17:15–18	39
9:1–2	8	12:7	41	17:36	77
9:3	8	13:1–21:42	50	18:1–19:48	8, 12
9:4–14	8	13:1–19:51	13	18:1	44
9:9–11	80	13:1–33	12, 66	18:3	42
9:14	10, 60, 71, 77	13:1–7	8, 17–18, 77	18:4	43
9:15	8, 10	13:1	10, 17, 31, 38,	18:6	44
9:16–21	8		41, 48, 58	18:7	25, 38, 66
9:22–23	8	13:2–6	38	18:9	57
9:23	71	13:6	42–43, 93	18:10	44
9:24–27	8	13:7	43	19:9	43
9:24	25	13:8–33	8	19:47	41
9:26	10	13:8	25, 38, 43	19:49–50	8, 38
9:27	30	13:13	31, 41	19:51	8, 10, 28, 44
10:1–5	8	13:14	38, 43, 60, 66	20:1–21:42	13
10:1–2	47, 80	13:15	38	20:1–9	9–10
10:1	71	13:24	38	20:1–6	77
10:6–14	8	13:29	38	20:1–2	59
10:8	37, 58, 77	13:33	38, 43, 60, 66	20:8	66
10:10	89	14:1–19:48	43	20:30	37
10:11	89	14:1–17:18	12	20:32	37

21:1–42   9–10, 33, 38, 43, 66
21:1   28,
21:2   60
21:4   61
21:7   66
21:8   61
21:12   39
21:14–16   104–5
21:36–39   66
21:43–45   9, 13, 17–18, 104
21:43   37, 39, 41, 114
21:44   49, 114
21:45   61
22:1–24:28   13
22:1–34   13, 67
22:1–4   67
22:1–6   13, 18
22:1–8   9
22:2   10, 25
22:3   32
22:4   41, 49
22:4–5   25
22:5   55, 67, 77–78, 101, 115
22:6–8   67
22:7–34   13
22:9–34   9
22:9   41, 67
22:10–34   10
22:13   28
22:14   28
22:17   32
22:19–20   67
22:19   41
22:20   47
22:21   28
22:30–31   28
22:31   109
23:1–24:28   13–14, 20, 71
23:1–16   9, 18, 49, 62, 71
23:1   17, 31, 49
23:2   27
23:5   42, 62
23:6   56, 62
23:7   56
23:8–9   32
23:8   41

23:9   41
23:11   55, 71, 115
23:12–13   41
23:13   39
23:14–15   39
23:15–16   77
23:15   39, 62
23:16   71
23:44–45   92
24:1–28   9, 18, 20, 49, 72, 99, 112
24:2–13   62, 77
24:3   113
24:4   39, 113
24:5   114
24:7–8   113
24:7   113–14
24:9–10   113
24:11–13   114
24:13–18   39
24:13   39, 114
24:14–24   62
24:14   113
24:15–16   32
24:16–18   72, 99
24:19–20   95, 112
24:19   32, 103
24:24   112
24:26   56–57
24:28   43
24:29–33   9, 13–14
24:29   26
24:31   27
24:33   28

Judges   20, 33, 49
1:1–36   31
1:9–20   31
2:1–5   31
2:10   27
2:20–23   31
3:1–4   31
3:1–2   45
3:11   49
4   89
5:31   49
6:11–16   106
8:28   49
21:25   27

1 Samuel   20
1:18   57

7   89
15   48
17:26   83
17:37   106

2 Samuel   20
3:18   26
7:1   49
7:8   26
7:9–11   49
7:9   106
7:13   50
14:17   49

1 Kings   20
8:12–13   57
8:23   80
8:53   25
8:56   25, 50
11:1–8   92
11:13   26
14:18   25–26
16:31   92
20:30–43   92
21:3   43

2 Kings   20
17:13   25–26
17:37   53
18:12   25
19: 4   83
19 :26   83
19:34   26
21:8   25
21:8–15   26
22–23   24, 53
23:25–28   26

2 Chronicles
1:3   25
24:6   25

Nehemiah
1:7–8   25

Psalms
18:47   83
42:3   83
83:1   49
84:3   83
86:2   26

97:5	84	Jeremiah		Micah		
114:7	84	10:10	83	4:13	84
116:7	49	18:18	51	6:15	40
116:16	26	23:26	83			
123:2	26	45:3	49	Haggai		
132:8	49	49:1–2	40	2:11–13	51

Proverbs		Ezekiel		Zechariah		
1:8	51	7:26	51	4:14	84
4:4	51			6:5	84
4:11	51	Daniel				
13:14	51	6:21	83	Malachi		
16:33	44			3:22	25
		Hosea				
		2:1	83			
Isaiah		4:6	51	Matthew		
8:16	51			22:34–40	55
28:12	49	Jonah				
53	26	1:7	44			

OTHER LITERATURE

NASB   New American Standard Bible